ADVENTURES IN MANIFESTING

ADVENTURES IN MANIFESTING

SUCCESS AND SPIRITUALITY

Sarah Prout and Sean Patrick Simpson

The Adventures In Manifesting series: Volume #1.

First published 2011 by Älska Publishing

Office based in Melbourne, Australia

Typeset in Giovanni LT 9/12/14 pt

© Sarah Prout and Sean Patrick Simpson

The moral rights of the authors have been asserted.

National Library of Australia Cataloguing-in-Publishing entry:

Authors:	Prout, Sarah 1979 – / Simpson, Sean Patrick 1984 –
Title:	Adventures In Manifesting: Success and Spirituality
ISBN:	9780987162908 (pbk)
Subjects:	Self help, New Age Publications, Inspiration
Dewey Number:	158.1

Cover design by Sarah Prout

Editorial revisions in house

Printed in Hong Kong

Also available in electronic format

*note that grammar and US/UK English is reflected in each author's preferred writing style.

www.AlskaPublishing.com

Disclaimer
The material in this publication is of the nature of general comment only and does not represent professional advice. To the maximum extent permitted by the law, the authors and publisher disclaim all responsibility and liability to any person, arising directly or indirectly from any person taking or not taking action based upon the information in this publication.

Älska means to LOVE

(Say it like this: *elsh-ka*)

This book is dedicated to people that aspire to live with Love

CONTENTS

ACKNOWLEDGMENTS

With boundless gratitude we would like to thank all of the Älska authors for sharing their amazing stories of inspiration. We would also like to thank our students in the **AdventuresInManifesting.org** community and *you* (the reader) for supporting the Älska vision of Love and Oneness.

From Sarah:

I would like to thank my beautiful children that I love with all my heart – Thomas and Olivia. Your presence in my life is truly appreciated beyond words. Being your mother is the greatest gift I have ever been given. Eternal thanks and kisses to Sean Patrick Simpson (I love you so much) and Älska– you are a pleasure to work with. Heartfelt thanks Joan and Mollie – thank you for making me feel so loved. To my family that I cherish dearly –Tony Prout, Louise Findlay, Henrietta Prout, Dave Frazer and Reuben Crossman. Thanks to my dear friends Sri Bhai Sahib ji and fellow meditation family (Joy, Donna, Pete, Dave, Ross). Special thanks to Rebecca Lange, Bronya Wilkins, Jill McGuire, Jenny Butler, Ben Capp, Sally Guillén, Nina Springle, Alan the crow, Red Mango man, Louise Hay, Abel Allen, Ursula Gestefeld, Dr. Marilyn Joyce my family and everyone that I have shared laughter with over the years. With LOVE, love and more love – thank you! xoxo

From Sean:

To my twin flame Sarah Prout – you are my greatest manifestation. To Mom and Dad – Thank you for all of your love. You two are amazing. To Noni, Kyla and Bradley – I just want to wrap you in my arms and hug you. To Scott and Dallyce – Words can not express the gratitude I have for you. Thank you for being the beautiful lights that you are. To my Crew – You are family and in my heart always. To Ryan – You've been traveling this journey right with me brother. Keep it rockin' homie.

To Justin – over thirty-one million listeners brother. We'll make it another hundred million to hear our music. To Martin – great work on the books man. To Thomas and Olivia - thank you for all you've taught me. To some of my greatest inspirations I have yet to meet and befriend in loving joy: Oprah, Ellen, Will Smith, Jim Carrey, Tony Robbins and Richard Branson. Thank you for *being* and inspiring the world through not just what you do, but who you are. You are beautiful souls.

To all my friends, mentors, guides and family: you are my greatest blessings. I am truly lucky to be on a journey that is filled with so many beautiful souls. Thank you for each and everyone of you. *I love you all.*

INTRODUCTION

Älska

It is with soul-felt gratitude that we would like to welcome you to the *Adventures in Manifesting* series. It has been designed as a source you will continuously enjoy reading when in search of insight, wisdom and inspiration. The stories are shared from people just like you that are on a wondrous journey of self-discovery.

From a multitude of unique vantage points, these stories demonstrate active examples of inner guidance, connection, faith and love that has transcended all limitations. Each story has been written with you in mind.

Reading with Your Soul

Our advice to you is that you read with an open heart, an open mind and absorb the information that sparks your own adventure in manifesting. When reading from a place of wonderment and curiosity, you are bound to find deep resonance. Ask yourself, what here resonates with me? What inspired action am I being guided to take? What can I learn from this now? Allow yourself to find a connection point within each story and within yourself that is right for you.

Your Own Treasure Map

While you will discover truths that each author has found for themselves, you can find in-between the lines your own truths as well. The wonder of this book is that understanding and resonating with certain concepts will happen at different points in your life. So take your time. Keep the book by your bedside table. Pick it up when you feel inspired and follow your inner guidance to the story you're meant to draw from now. Whether you read through it all in one sitting, or piece-by-piece, you will find this a place of inspiration for years to come.

The Mission of Älska

The mission of Älska is to bestow the teachings of Love and Oneness and proliferate its message throughout the world. Within these two illuminated concepts is the power of vibrancy, creativity, joy and inspiration. While the mechanisms of metaphysical principles here have been in place since the dawn of time, it is our purest intention to continue this work that began to gain prominence at the beginning of the 19th century in the New Thought Movement.

What are you Manifesting?

You may have noticed on the front cover this very powerful question. Ask yourself this to begin reading with some basic intentions and ideas of what you desire. Just as we would teach you, we are *acting as if* and actively demonstrating how to imprint the Universe with the vibration of success, thus the questions.

In the years before Jim Carrey became a superstar, he wrote himself a check for $10 million dollars and added "for acting services rendered". He carried it in his wallet from that day forth until the abundance and recognition that he desired started to manifest in his life. This act of setting an almighty intention contributed to his success eventually growing to fruition. As witnessed, the Universe responds to what is radiated energetically.

Your Journey Begins Now

Start it from a place of love and gratitude, knowing that as you read you will find resonance with what you are in alignment with in this point of time.

You will find yourself beginning to develop a story through direct experience of your intended reality. As you do, we will be here waiting with expectant joy and an open heart to see what you have to share with the world as well.

Until then, we will look forward to hearing all about your own adventures in manifesting.

With Love and Gratitude,
Älska

About Älska

Älska is the combined energies of Sarah Prout and Sean Patrick Simpson. The company name means 'Love' and was received as gentle guidance one evening after a very intense session of laughter and joy.

You say it like this: 'elsh-ka' – which is slightly different than the original Scandinavian pronunciation of their verb (which means 'to Love').

Sean and Sarah were prompted from within to start a metaphysical publishing company based on their mutual adoration of Universal truth and passion for writing. Hence, Älska was created!

http://www.AlskaPublishing.com

SHARE YOUR EXPERIENCE

Has a particular story, insight or teaching stood out to you?

We'd love to hear about your experience, so feel free to get in touch and let us know. You can e-mail us at:

feedback@whatareyoumanifesting.com

Additionally, with the intention and desire to share stories and teachings from all walks of life, we'd like to invite you to potentially be a part of one of the next *Adventures in Manifesting* titles.

Stories of all topics about manifesting are welcome (success, spirituality, health, happiness, wealth, love, prosperity, inner guidance, achieving dreams, overcoming obstacles, etc.)

If chosen as a top submission, we will get in touch directly to invite you to be a part of one of our next *Adventures in Manifesting* titles.

Please go to www.WhatAreYouManifesting.com to share your experience (not to mention join the course and community, as well as find the hard copy, Kindle and iBook versions of other titles in the series).

Enjoy!

THE POWER OF QUESTIONS, PRESENCE AND THE COSTUME OF LIFE

Sean Patrick Simpson

I am protected. My parents and elders know best. All I have to do is what I'm told. Though I may not like it all the time, they know best and know what's right...

Remember this – that time of magic and wonderment in which you were guided and told what is right and wrong, good or bad? You were given all the answers, right? It was a pretty simple way of life. You ask your parents or someone older than you a question, and you get an answer and automatically believe it to be true.

I vaguely remember that time of acceptance of whatever I was told. However, more strongly I remember discovering something else going on. Those I looked to for guidance didn't have all the answers as I once thought.

Who Has the Answers?

Years ago when I became a teenager and the idea that adults had all the answers began to wear off. I began to notice a common theme that the dramas, frustrations, irritations, annoyances – anything that 'bothered' an adult didn't seem any different than that of teenagers. Whether they were in their twenties, thirties, forties, or older, the same experiences happened over and over again.

I didn't understand. *Shouldn't they have manifested more presence? Shouldn't they have manifested more peace within? If they had these experiences as kids, why do they still have them?* It just didn't make sense to me why adults would continue going through internal upheaval year after year, when all that had to be done was the asking of simple questions and a willingness to receive the answers.

I decided that if I were to experience dramas and frustrations in childhood, I wouldn't want to have it a reoccurring theme through old age. I wanted to manifest ongoing peace, happiness and joy in life. Thus, a question was born that would *continuously* change my life over and over again. We'll get to that question in a moment, but first...

Manifesting Presence: Where Attention Goes, Energy Flows

Remember that cliché? Kind of cheesy, right? For now, consider releasing thoughts and feelings of, "I've heard that before."

If you've heard it and know it, but aren't embodying it, then you're not truly 'getting it.'

Getting it is more than just intellectual understanding. *It's experiential understanding* through practice – an ideal I think all of us should strive towards.

Recently, a student from our AdventuresInManifesting.org community was asking for some guidance that embodies this concept of 'where attention goes, energy flows' – wanting to manifest more presence within himself as well.

"I spend two hours each day driving to work, feeling totally disconnected and frustrated. The traffic is a pain in the ass. I know it doesn't have to be that way so I'm trying to overcome this mindset," he said. "How can I get around this experience that is loaded with disharmony?"

Great question. And here's my response: "Sounds like you've got a couple hours a day to practice and focus on conscious gratitude bud. This isn't about the 'external experience' (traffic), which will show up in infinite ways throughout life. It's about the 'internal experience' (your response), which you have the ability to control.

Right now you're the victim of your internal reactions and are having *contracting feelings* (frustration, irritation, anger, etc). However, if you consciously choose the direction to where your attention goes, your energy can flow towards *expanding feelings* (presence, joy, love, gratitude, stillness, etc) and thus have a much more enjoyable experience every single day.

You only have a limited amount of 'space' you can fill up in your conscious awareness. So the question becomes, 'Why fill it up with anything less than positive?'

Thoughts become things, and if in the moment you're unable to think of anything that's good, then you have the opportunity for an even deeper level of experience – the silent surrender of thought and mind. But that's another story..."

As he listened, he really began to 'get it.' There was still one thing missing though: practical tools to help him when in the midst of the experience that would help him to manifest a better outcome.

It's all fine and dandy to suggest everyone to 'just think positive thoughts,' but if our mind is already running on tangents that don't serve us, then we could use some help in guiding us. This is where we come back full swing to the questions I said earlier would continuously change my life over and over again...

What am I supposed to learn from this experience? What's the lesson in this and how can I grow from it?

In my friend's case, the answers ranged from learning how to consciously focus his mind on the things he felt joy and happiness towards (gratitude), as well as practicing more patience and surrender in life. Is it possible that had he been asking these questions twenty years ago, he wouldn't be having the negative experiences he has now?

When we don't learn the lesson we're meant to from an experience, the Universe will slap it right back at us, over and over and over again until the day we die or until we 'get it.'

Next time you're having an experience that charges negative feelings within, ask yourself what the lesson is and how you can grow from it. Then, quiet down and listen. Trust the answers will manifest themselves through surrender. It may be a specific answer like those suggested above, or one that is even less noticeable, which you've been guided to from an even 'deeper source' than the mind.

Quality Questions

If you look back on your life where you've had the greatest amount of growth, you may likely find there was a common theme: You were asking questions – questions to yourself, questions to others, and maybe even questions to God.

> *"The quality of your life is in direct proportion to the quality of the questions you ask yourself."* – Tony Robbins

The question "What's the lesson in this and how can I grow from it?" is one of those 'quality questions' I would recommend writing down to add to your arsenal. Additionally, the key is to constantly look for ways in which you can improve the quality of your questions. Are the questions you ask yourself and others empowering or disempowering?

'How can I improve?' vs. 'Why can't I get anything right?'

The right questions can lead you to a place of more and more presence, help you let go of ideas and preconceived beliefs that have bound you to the shackles of drama, and gradually guide you towards a deeper place of love.

The Costume of Life: Manifesting Who We Really Are

A few years ago, I was pointed in the direction of a concept that really shook up my perceptions and understandings of life, myself and people in general.

What it did was show me a much deeper level of understanding, love and compassion towards the perspectives, viewpoints and 'truths' held by others. Essentially, it got me 'outside' of myself and willing to consider the possibility that *my way* was *not the only way*, or necessarily *the right way.*

It was suggested to me that in this life, we are more than just a human being occasionally having a spiritual experience, but are more alike to spiritual beings having a human experience, all the time. *We are much more than we appear to be.*

In a sentence, the idea is that *we are all merely wearing costumes in this life,* masking our eternal essence, and even forgetting about it. I'll explain...

Think of an actor playing a role on stage. Is the actor actually *the character* they're portraying? Of course not. What if, though, the actor became so identified with their role that they forgot who they really are? What if after the show they got off the stage and went about life actually thinking they were the character they were playing, with the same history, desires, characteristics, behaviors and thought patterns?

This, I propose, is what many of us tend to do. Bound by our definitions, experiences and views of the world, we lose sight of our higher self – *who we truly are*. Incidentally, seeing them only as their 'character' and ready to condemn them for any mistakes that conflict with the beliefs of our own 'character', we forget *who others truly are* as well.

Each and every person's 'character' is simply the sum total of their thoughts and experiences in life. Is it possible that you'd be no different than anyone else had you grown up in the same place, with the same family, friends, teachings, conditions and experiences?

Be Willing to Release Your Costume

I would invite you to 'try on', as you would a piece of clothing, this new way of viewing the world and people around you. See them simply as actors playing a role, realizing that many, if not most, have simply *forgotten who they truly are*. As an observer, you need not get pulled into their dramas but simply watch in detached entertainment like you would any show, with a sense of newfound understanding, compassion and love as to what they deem as their own 'truth'.

From this place, you can now maintain *your* truth, but understand, respect, and appreciate how and why they've developed *their* truth – no matter how different or conflicting it is to yours.

As you witness, stand outside your own self as well. Become witness to the fact that any opinions or conclusions you make about their character is solely based on the perspective of *your own role* (the sum total of all your thoughts and experiences), which by definition will be a limited point of view.

You are more than just your actions. You are more than just your ideas. You are more than just your mind, ego and identity. And the same goes for everyone whose path intertwines with your own. Be willing to release the costume you cling to so you can manifest and see who you and others *really are*. Each and every one of us is a presence beyond that which we can see, beyond all thought and form and an observing, thriving soul of love and curiosity.

Embodiment of All You Will Learn and Your Own Adventures in Manifesting

You, my friend, are about to embark on an incredible journey that is filled with new insights and understandings. Already, you may potentially begin perceiving the world in entirely new ways – and that is just through one chapter, with a few new tools for manifesting a more joyful life.

Here within the contents of this book are many journeys to be inspired from, with each author sharing the truth they've discovered for themselves.

Just remember that *each person's truth is their own*. Some you may resonate with, others you may not. The important thing to do is to *'use' your mind to seek inspiration* while *'allowing' your soul to guide you*. By doing this, you will find exactly what you need to assist you on your own journey.

Remember to ask empowering questions:

- *What am I supposed to learn from this experience?*

- *What's the lesson in this and how can I grow from it?*

And finally, realize that by seeing through the costume of life, you will begin to experience a constant reminder of who you and others *truly are*. You'll find the ability to turn even those you may consider 'unlikable' into your greatest gift, your greatest lesson and your greatest source of inspiration.

About the Author

Sean Patrick Simpson is the Co-Founder of Älska Publishing, author and speaker of topics such as mindset, language patterns, metaphysics and spirituality. A musician and singer at heart, he has had his compositions played for over 31 million people internationally.

Through a rich love and soul journey that's been part of him long before this life, he tends to attract the most beautiful of friendships, companions, teachers and students, all of whom he loves dearly. Raised in Orange County, California with a particular fondness for the San Diego and Los Angeles regions, he now resides in Melbourne, Australia with his beautiful love and twin flame Sarah Prout.

Sean is not only a teacher, but a *listener* who seeks to find truth within everyone.

With a dedication and commitment to being perfectly aligned with his most joyful self, he is quite content when found spontaneously silly dancing, singing in the midst of public gatherings and jamming to music that inspires his soul (whether it be pop/dance, jazz, classical or choral works of the contemporary, baroque and renaissance eras).

Sean absolutely thrives when performing on stage or speaking to a crowd – whether it be through a song in his heart or words of inspiration.

http://www.AdventuresInManifesting.org

http://www.SeanPatrickSimpson.com

THE TRIPTYCH OF MANIFESTING

Sarah Prout

My adventures in manifesting so far have been a wondrous journey that continues to unravel soul-stirring levels of gratitude, laced with reverential praise and spirited awe, in my life.

Your Connection to Love Is Your Own Private Universe

As I write these words, I want to emphasise that it is truth written from *my own* personal viewpoint. In no way do I claim to have all the answers. I'll tell you that in my more gentle moments, I've been an absolute bitch in my quest to feel *right* in the past. And if you can keep a secret, I'll admit that I've even been a nightmare to some of the people I love the most. The only reason I want to admit this is because my strongest desire is to give you a message of hope and spark creativity within your heart – which I can only do from a place of *authenticity*. We all screw things up from time to time, and each new moment can become an opportunity to grow a little more. An open heart and the ability to laugh at yourself can be the best soul medicine this planet has to offer.

I'm still learning to step back and look at events that challenge me from a place of Love. Ironically, my dedication to practising this intention keeps presenting many opportunities that prove my willingness and congruency.

Cultivating *your own truth* is a beautiful process. The good, the bad, and the downright ugly – it's all exquisite and uniquely yours.

The Ineffable Beauty of Success and Spirituality Is to Nurture Our Connection to the Divine Within

Sikhs refer to the *Divine within* as the omniscient, omnipotent force that is all pervading, beyond the endless cycles of birth and death. It's the essence of love that permeates everything in the Cosmos.

This description of the truly *incomprehensible fabric* that binds our Universe is what I have found to resonate with the strongest in my life so far. *Love is all there is.* God, the Source, the Universe, the Force, Chi or the Naam is animating and orchestrating everything in conjunction with the vibrations, thoughts and feelings we are offering on a moment-to-moment basis.

Manifesting occurs when your desires and intentions are in perfect alignment with this greater force that fuels our existence.

If you've studied The Law of Attraction before, then you'll be familiar with the three-step process of manifesting your desires: *asking, allowing* and *receiving*. While I completely believe in these three steps, I feel there is a greater depth that needs to be explored and expanded upon further – what I feel is the triptych of manifesting.

Love, Surrender and Gratitude

1. **Love** is the golden thread that runs through us all. It's our connection to the life force that is in everything. It is the power that holds the planets in alignment, the stars in the sky, and the water in the ocean. The power resides in unconditional love for ourselves: families and all human beings and creatures. I love the quote: *"Show me where God is not?"*

2. **Surrender** is the process where you can get out of the way of your thoughts and feel present and connected to the Love. The pure act of cultivating presence through surrender is intimated in all of the scriptures from all of the world's religions. Surrender is the best form of reverence and communion with the Divine. There's a stillness that happens when you just let go and surrender. It's like a magic that unfolds to show it's the path of least resistance that will comfort you the most. Think of the moments each night just before you fall asleep. The thoughts

slow, you relax and drift into a state of rejuvenation. When you surrender through meditation, your life experience will mirror the Love in direct proportion to what you're offering. In fact, what I've observed is that everything in life tends to operate like a giant mirror. Whatever you put out there will be projected back and magnified. *Radiate love and love will beam back at you.*

3. **Gratitude** is the driving force. It shows the Universe you're connected to the creative experience and enjoying every step of the way. Appreciation is the best state to approach all of life's lessons. The truest levels of grace and spirituality are the abilities to look beyond the situation and beneath the surface. From there, you can uncover the pure beauty of things and thank them for teaching you.

When Doubt Creeps In

William Shakespeare once said that our doubts are our traitors. What I believe is that thoughts become things, so why does my mind still ask silly questions that don't serve me?

What do I really believe? How can I teach people about spirituality when I don't consistently love myself? Am I a teacher? I don't feel like a teacher; I feel like a faker. How can I write authentically about success and spirituality?

When I opened my computer to attempt another writing session of the chapter you are reading now, an email flew into my inbox that left me in tears. It was from a man that was writing to me for advice. He had survived cancer, had two small children, and when he read my book 'The Power of Influence'. He ended his message by saying: *"Halos of a thousand angels to you for all you have done and what you do to help others."*

In that moment, even though I was struggling to keep my head above water emotionally that day, I felt immense gratitude that in one person's life I had made a small difference. It made me feel humbled by the power of words and how expressing appreciation to others has such healing and transformational energy behind it.

What would flow next as I continued to write were three powerful snippets of *life*, *love* and *guidance* to remind both you and I the power of manifesting…

Manifesting Life

When I was twenty, I lost a baby. For four months, there was a heartbeat, and then it stopped. I don't think I really understood how fragile life was until it was there, and then it wasn't. My soul felt lost for a few months. During this time, I immersed myself in meditation and in trying to be present in order to rise above the pain. The doctor told me that I could try to get pregnant again (if I wanted) in six months after my body had recovered from the trauma of losing the baby. However, less than six weeks later, two little pink lines on the pregnancy test showed up and my son Thomas was on his way.

In August 2001, after thirty-four hours of chronic cycles of pain, my baby was dragged out of me and plonked onto my chest. This tiny human being peered up at me with these *all-knowing* cloudy-blue eyes, as he wrapped his entire hand around my little finger. I felt the most intense feeling of love for this child. It was a primal force that just seemed to appear out of nowhere. Here I was, a twenty-one-year-old mother that had barely any life experience myself, now entrusted to care for this old soul that had appeared from the unseen to the seen for me to love, grow with, and learn from.

Manifesting Love

I was married for nearly ten years. After two children, many adventures, and a heart that drifted in a different direction, it ended in divorce. Little did I know that on my quest to create a new story for myself, I would manifest true love from the other side of the planet.

"I'm going to put a message in a bottle, throw it in the ocean and see if it gets to the person I want to send it to one day." – @sarahprout via Twitter, October 1st 2009. I was having a moment where I wondered if I would ever fall in love.

"Sarah, I'll be sure to go to the beach every day and look for a bottle then." –@vpsean (Sean Patrick Simpson) replied via Twitter on the same day.

Less than a year later, Sean and I were kissing and holding each other on the beautiful beaches of Noosa, Australia. Here I was, with a perfect stranger from Los Angeles, California that I met online (on Twitter!) and as soon as he stepped off the plane, we felt like we had known one another for eons upon eons.

The day we met, the most enormous rainbow I have ever seen in my life appeared when we were driving home. More vibrant and bright than any spectrum of colours I have ever witnessed, it felt like a sign that we were meant to be together and that I had indeed manifested true love.

This new chapter in my life with Sean feels brilliantly illuminated. I am so in awe of his presence and how amazing he is with my children. It takes a phenomenal amount of grace to help raise a child that is not of your own blood. I know this myself from becoming a stepmother when I was nineteen. Now the tables have turned and I have this man in my life that is filled with so much love, that it can extend to benefit my children as well.

His courage is strength personified, and the selflessness is something that aspiring Masters seek to acquire in lifetime after lifetime. Every day I wake up next to him and feel like the luckiest lady in the world. Daily life is like a true reminder of the power of manifesting.

Manifesting Guidance

A true connection to Oneness is to listen to guidance as it is presented. The more you pay attention to your level of discernment, the more strength and accuracy will be presented to you.

One afternoon, Sean was driving the car as we were picking up the children from school and running late.

"How about you jump out and I'll park the car?" he said.

As I reached for the door handle, a voice within said 'STOP'. Pausing, I suddenly saw a large bus speed past us. If I hadn't stopped and paused when I did, I would have been killed instantly (or at least very badly squished).

I felt shocked by the close call. With gratitude, I was reminded that we all must listen to the gentle guidance, angels and higher energies that whisper to protect us in hours (and sometimes split seconds) of need.

In conclusion, I believe that success and spirituality are in full force when you understand your mission is in combination with love, surrender and gratitude. Your greatest manifesting power resides in your creative energy being totally in flow. When your heart and mind are vibrating with love and excitement for everything life is presenting you with, then you are living life on purpose and enjoying your exquisite adventure in manifesting.

About the Author

Sarah Prout is a bestselling author, award-winning entrepreneur, lover of metaphysics and Co-Founder and Creative Director of Älska Publishing.

With a strong background in art, design and literature – Sarah's combined passions for publishing, online connection and writing have gained international recognition and media attention on a global scale.

Anything with a twist of ornateness, a quirky play on words, a glimmer of Universal truth or a rampage of silliness will capture her heart with awe and inspiration. She believes that you create your own reality with your thoughts and feelings and that nothing feels better than laughing until your face hurts.

She lives in Melbourne, Australia with her twin flame love Sean Patrick Simpson and her two beautiful children.

http://www.SarahProut.com

SEVEN WAYS TO ATTRACT MORE MONEY

Joe Vitale

Want to attract more money?

Wondering why you haven't attracted it when you've done everything you thought you needed to do?

What really works when it comes to attracting more money, anyway?

I've been studying the Law of Attraction for more than three decades. I've written several books about it, including 'The Attractor Factor' and 'The Key'. That's why I ended up in the movie The Secret, and then on Larry King and Donny Deutsch's television shows, among others. I know how the Law of Attraction works, and I know why so many people don't clearly understand it.

When it comes to the Law of Attraction, most people want to learn how to use it to attract more money first. After that, they'll wonder how to attract romance, cars, homes, happiness, and everything else. But money is the starting place for most people.

So, how do you attract more money?

When it comes to attracting anything -- and money in particular -- there are seven ways to do it right. Here they are:

1. Give Money Away

It sounds counter-intuitive but the more you give, the more you will receive (unless you block the receiving, which ties into the next step). Give openly and freely to wherever you received spiritual nourishment. Give on a regular basis, too. The rule of thumb is to give 10% of whatever you receive, but it's also smart to give more when you feel inspired to do so.

Remember, give to the person, place, or group that has kept your spirit alive. Just ask "Where was I most inspired this past·week?" and give to that source. And ask the question daily or weekly as the source will often change.

Here's an inside tip: When most people give money, they do it with a tight fist. They don't give much. Why not? Because they're afraid. They're holding on. Well, the energy of fear will attract more things to fear. Instead, give money with an open heart and an expectation of return. *Give in love.*

2. Get Clear

Most people push money away with their hidden limiting beliefs, such as "money is bad" or "rich people are evil." Those are beliefs, not facts. Get clear of them and money will come to you (as long as you also do the next step).

Getting clear is truly "The Missing Secret" to making the Law of Attraction work for you all the time. After all, it isn't your conscious intentions that are being manifested in your life, it is your un-conscious counter-intentions.

For example, when you set a goal on New Year's Day to stop smoking or date more, what happened the next week? You gave up your conscious goal for your un-conscious belief that you couldn't do it. You weren't in alignment with your intention. You werent' "clear."

Most likely in your unconscious mind you have limiting beliefs about money, such as -

a. "Money is evil."
b. "Money will attract problems."
c. "Money will make me a selfish person."
d. "Wanting money is greedy."
e. "Rich people are snobs."

If you have one or more of those limiting beliefs within you, do you really think you'll attract any money? In truth, you'll attract NOT having money.

Why? Because your unconscious counter-intention ("Money is bad") will veto your conscious intention ("I now attract more money into my life").

Is it any wonder some people say the movie The Secret or the Law of Attraction doesn't work? Obviously, once you clear those hidden blocks/beliefs to your success, your success has nothing in the way of happening. The roadblocks are gone.

I talk about ways to get clear in my new audio program, "The Missing Secret." One thing you can do right now is to simply question your beliefs. Become a belief detective and look for those limiting beliefs about money. When you release your inner blocks, you will attract more money.

3. Take Action

Too many people sit and wait for money to materialize in front of them. I believe in magic and miracles, but I also believe that your role in the process of attracting money is to actually do something to bring it your way. Act on your ideas. Now. "Money likes speed" is my favorite mantra.

If you don't act now, you'll see your idea manifested in a store some day and somebody else will be attracting money from it. What can you do right now, today, to move toward creating something that will attract more money?

Whatever it is, do it.

When you doubt and second-guess yourself instead of taking action, you are demonstrating that you aren't yet clear (see second tip above) about money and your right to attract it. Act now and get rich.

4. Support a Cause

Most people push money away because they don't feel they deserve it. One way around this (while you still work on getting clear inside yourself) is to want money for a larger purpose. I created Operation YES to end homelessness. Raising hundreds of thousands of dollars (or more) for that cause will remove any remaining prosperity limitations within me. While I won't receive a dime from Operation YES, my working on its behalf will attract money to me in other ways, such as the contacts and goodwill I'll create.

In short, want money for a larger reason than your own ego. This is a beautiful way to attract more money without wanting it only for yourself. Realize that when you are wealthy, you are better able to help family, friends, your community, and even the world. A good reason to attract more money is for all the good it can do for others, not just you. Ask yourself what cause would you support (or even create) once you attracted more money?

5. Get Support

One of the wisest things you can do to achieve any goal is create or join a mastermind group devoted to it. I co-authored Meet and Grow Rich with Bill Hibbler for this reason: to teach you how to create a support group.

The idea is to be around people who can keep your energy and inspiration high. While you can make progress alone, it's so much easier when you have support.

This support can also come in the way of audiotapes, books, and other learning tools. I've been buying audios from Nightingale-Conant for more than thirty years for just that reason: it helps me stay focused on constantly growing and improving. Even when I was struggling, I went to the library and borrowed books and tapes to keep me informed and inspired. Today I can afford to buy my own materials, but it's only because I invested in my education every step along the way.

I created "The Missing Secret" audio set to help people understand the practical use of the Law of Attraction. Again, all of this is support in helping you attract more money.

6. Be Grateful

This is huge. Be thankful for the money you have – which is probably considered true wealth by people starving in third world countries – and you'll begin to attract more money. Gratitude sends off a signal of appreciation, which brings to you more to be thankful for. Begin with whatever is in this moment that you can be sincerely grateful for.

After I was homeless and while I was still experiencing poverty, I began this exercise by holding a pencil and being grateful for it. Once I truly experienced gratitude, it shifted my energy vibe so I could then experience more to be grateful for. Today I have much to be thankful for – from houses to cars to collectible guitars -- but it all began with a pencil.

Look around and ask yourself what you are grateful for right now. Then get into that feeling.

7. Do what you Love

There's no sense in working at something you hate. If you are currently at a job you don't like, find a way to enjoy it for the time you are there while working towards doing your passion. Following your passion is the greatest secret of all when it comes to attracting wealth.

Everyone from Donny Deutsch to Donald Trump to Bill Gates to little ole me agree that passion (combined with the other steps above) is your ticket to financial freedom. Even when I worked for oil companies back in Houston and didn't like my work, I found ways to do what I loved. I wrote my first book on my lunch hours. I spoke on weekends and sold my book in the back of the room. Over time, doing what I love became my life. And today it's my moment-by-moment wonder.

Ask yourself what you would do even if you were never paid. That's a clue to what you should be doing and of course finding a way to be paid for it. You can attract more money from love.

Finally, expect success.

The mindset of expectation – expecting that you are now attracting money and playfully looking around, asking "I wonder how big money will come to me today?" – will keep your brain turned on to seek and find opportunities. You of course then have to take fearless action when you see them.

Go for it!

About the Author

Dr. Joe Vitale is the author of way too many books to list here and featured teacher on The Secret. His latest title is "The Attractor Factor: 5 Easy Steps for Creating Wealth (or anything else) From the Inside Out."

http://www.mrfire.com

THE QUAKE OF TRANSFORMATION

Marilyn Joyce

A morning I will never forget: January 17th 1994! I woke up with a start ten minutes later than usual. I dashed out of bed and hurriedly took a shower to get ready for work. I had never slept in or been late to my job. That morning, I realized and accepted that no matter what, I would be a few minutes late. Oh well…

In an instant, being late was the least of my problems! My world turned upside down. One minute I was standing in front of my open refrigerator, and the next minute, I was pinned under my refrigerator, experiencing agonizing pain. The 1994 Northridge earthquake hit us like a long drawn-out flash – up, down and sideways! It literally tore parts of our beautiful city apart, including my little section of West Los Angeles!

Fortunately my neighbors rushed in and freed me from the "attacking" refrigerator. But the carport, where my old beat-up duster was housed, completely collapsed on top of my car, which had the least possible insurance and was worth practically nothing to begin with. But it was my only mode of transportation in a city that had, at the time, an abominable transit system. My car was destroyed in an instant!

As it turned out, the ramp off the freeway I used daily to get to the office building where I worked had completely collapsed as well. In fact, so had the building! I guess you could say I was pretty darned lucky that this was the one day I happened to sleep in.

So there I was … No car, no job, and no home in a matter of seconds! Now what?

Fortunately I had friends close by, so I at least had a place to sleep until the building I lived in was repaired. The apartment however was never truly livable again after that quake.

Be Careful What You Ask for – And How You Ask for It!

What does this all have to do with adventures in manifesting? Well, a lot! I was constantly complaining about my apartment, its water leakage problems, and continuously talking about moving. My place however was convenient to *everything*. I was surrounded by lots of friends and it had become way too comfortable, despite the many water leakage problems! To be sure, one thing I have learned in life is that *you get what you ask for*. And if you're not specific about how you ask, you may not like the way it comes to you!

Agape to the Rescue

At the time, I was an active member of the Agape International Spiritual Center, tucked away on the border of Santa Monica and West Los Angeles. I lived within walking distance of my church and never missed a Sunday, Wednesday, and whatever other days something was going on there. I had just signed up to take the introductory course training to become a practitioner at Agape. However, following the earthquake I decided to cancel attending. After all, I had no place to live, no car and no income. When I met with Reverend Michael and a couple of the practitioners, they convinced me that this was exactly where I needed to be. And so the journey into manifestation began.

For the record, I have always manifested wonderful outcomes in my life – as well as some horrible outcomes along the way! *Remember what I stated earlier? You have to be careful what you ask for – and how you ask for the outcomes you desire. And do it with positive, specific, expectant, grateful and knowing intention.* I had never fully embraced this concept prior to my training at Agape.

You are Your Car in Los Angeles!

Obviously, I desperately needed a job. California is not an easy place to live if you have no income! I also needed a car ASAP. Being without a car keeps one stuck in a very small and limited part of this vast city. And of course, in Los Angeles, it used to be said (and maybe still is) that *you are your car*! I didn't believe that until a guy who was pursuing me ran the other way the moment he saw my old duster...

I'm getting ahead of myself though. Back to the sequence of events that began to unfold, after I was "talked into" going ahead with the classes...

First of all, I had to find a quiet place to work on the assignments and projects that were the foundation of the course. My girlfriend's home was chaotic to say the least, full of noisy kids and very little space, so Starbucks came to the rescue!

Getting Really Specific and Intentional...

In setting up my intentional plan, I determined that I first needed a job. But not just any job! It had to be a position where I was of *service* to others and a job I could truly and passionately embrace with all my heart and soul. It had to have a wide scope of autonomy, creativity, decision-making and responsibility in the development and implementation of programs and systems. It had to afford me the opportunity to speak, write and travel and provide me a great income. *Tall order, right?*

Secondly, I wanted a new car – one that was rust-free, always started up with the turn of the key, never broke down en route to anywhere, got great mileage (at least for that era), had a sunroof, automatic everything, and looked great! After all, I was in LA at the time and fell for that cliché, "You are your car!" *Shallow?* Perhaps I was at that time, a little... but heck, why not set the intention for what you *really* want?

Thirdly, I wanted an apartment that was convenient, clean, close to everything, and large enough for me to have an office at home, as well as space for living my life comfortably.

Finally, I was badly in need of some upscale clothes in my wardrobe. I had been living in jeans, sweat suits, and a few well-worn garments and shoes that really needed to be retired!

As you can see from my listed desires, my focus at that time was on *abundance*. I had my health in place, and overall, I generally experienced peace of mind and happiness, kind of living my life by choice, as the eye of the storm versus the storm!

Paint Your Life Picture

From my list of desires, I then created a mental picture by making a statement describing what it would look like if I had all these outcomes in place in the 'abundance' area of my life. I also included what I would *do* if I had more abundance, that I wasn't *doing* then, as well as how I would *be* in my life that I wasn't *being* then. Basically I painted my life picture!

Once all of this was written down, the spiritual mind treatments began, basically affirmative prayers of gratitude for what we have requested and already have. The steps (repeated at least three times daily) were as follows:

1. *Recognition:*   God is... (all there is!)

2. *Unification:*   I am... (one with God and all that exists)

3. *Realization:*   I want... (for the highest good of all concerned, including me)

4. *Thanksgiving:*   Thanks... (in advance knowing that it's already so)

5. *Release:*   Let Go and Let God!

Let the Miracles Begin

I have to tell you, what followed was nothing short of miraculous from my perspective. As much as I was very intellectually versed in the whole concept of manifestation, gratitude, prayer, belief, and intentional outcomes, I had never before been aware of such a simple and easy-to-implement process for designing my desired life.

Within two days of starting this process, I received a voicemail from the Cancer Treatment Centers of America (CTCA) requesting that I apply for the job of Director of Nutrition. I had conducted an extremely thought-provoking interview with Dr Carl O'Simonton who at the time facilitated a body-mind based program for CTCA, and who was one of the fathers of Psychoneuroimmunology. My article had been published in a national magazine, and CTCA was very impressed with what I had written and the depth of my insights into cancer care and treatments. Hence, they felt I was perfect for the job. A month earlier I had no interest in such a job, but at that moment, it seemed to be an answer to a prayer... if I got the job!

One very important question remained though... *How would I ever get to the job interview without a car?*

Remember, I had no vehicle, and the interview was an hour away if there was no traffic (California is notorious for traffic congestion!). Well, a girlfriend came to the rescue immediately and offered to pick me up on her way to work. She lived an hour away in the opposite direction too! Now, that's a real friend!

Within an hour of arriving home from the interview, I got a phone call confirming I got the job, including an *excellent* starting rate and awesome health insurance benefits! And they wanted me to start right away! There was only one problem – how would I get back and forth? Same girlfriend, same car to the rescue! I just had to arrange shorter workdays in the beginning to accommodate this transportation arrangement until I was able to get my own car. CTCA agreed to my terms.

No Credit, No Car Loan! What Next?

Just to set the record straight, I had no credit history to speak of at the time (another story in which I had just overcome a 5-year cancer journey a few years prior... shared in the *Adventures in Manifesting: Health & Happiness* title), no money saved up for a deposit on a car, and no credit cards to my name. What bank was going to even begin a conversation with me? That's when it got really interesting...

Out of the blue, an established businessman, who was the close friend of a doctor associate, heard of my situation and within a week, met with me and offered to co-sign on a car loan. He knew me from no one, yet he took me under his wings and introduced me to the bank manager at his bank! The manager and this businessman thought I was a great risk. And I proved them right! Within 3 weeks of starting my job, I had a spiffy new car with a sunroof, everything automatic, easy on gas, and a joy to drive!

A Different Story on the Home Front!

Next was the home part. The building got fixed where I had been living, so I went back temporarily (for a year) before moving into something bigger and more upscale. I simply didn't have the time nor interest to think about moving since my job became full-time in a very joyful way and in very short order! I was given almost complete autonomy to create, develop and implement new and innovative programs and systems. My position involved traveling and speaking all over the country and abroad. I was busy writing manuals and brochures for patient use. My income was immediately raised substantially, with a great travel expense account, plus my own personal cell phone (which back then was the size of a brick!), and every other perk imaginable. I had arrived!

With my great income and fabulous hot little car, I was able to find the best shopping places and outlet malls. Within six weeks of starting this spiritual mind treatment process, I had a brand new wardrobe that didn't even come close to breaking my newly expanding bank account.

So it all sounds pretty darned good up to this point, right? And it was! But this was only the beginning...

Appearing on TV and Creating My First Public Book...

Within eight months of riding this amazing crest and loving every minute of it – and yes, there were some tough moments as there always are when you're working with patients who are often terminally ill – I was asked to do six consecutive weekly TV segments on a nationally broadcast program that had more than *sixty million viewers*. The interviewer, a doctor, continually promoted a book that did not exist. When I tried to explain to her that I didn't have a book, only a patient manual, she told me to "just write the darned book!"

So out of that TV series came my first public book, *5 Minutes to Health*. Thousands of orders came from the first broadcasting of the six segments. It was so popular that they reran the series a number of times. And thousands more books were sold. I then took my books out on the road and spoke all over the world, writing other books, (*I Can't*

Believe It's Tofu!, Laugh at Stress and Love Life, and now, *INSTANT E.N.E.R.G.Y.™: The 5 Keys to Unlimited Energy & Vitality!*), collaborating in many others, and selling them literally everywhere I spoke.

Taking Control of my own Success

In complete frustration with the useless Public Relations firm I was paying a monthly fortune to, I finally decided to take control of my own PR program. I wanted to venture out and try less conventional approaches to media, so I began prayer treatments for this direction in my life. Within a few weeks of beginning this process, I had the good fortune of meeting Steve and Bill Harrison of Radio TV Interview Reports in the mid-nineties, and together, creating a mutually beneficial contract, I basically became my own PR rep while employing their incredible service. Radio and TV opportunities abounded and have kept me extremely busy for quite some time. As a result, life has been an amazing and delicious ride. And continues to be so…

Despite any challenges that life may throw my way – and let's face it, no one is immune to challenges! – *it's not what happens to us that counts, but how we relate to what happens.* I am thrilled to be alive! I love my life! I love the people in my life! And I look forward to every opportunity to make a difference in someone's life and on the planet.

Always remember that we are all from *the One Source, God,* and whatever we do must be for the *highest good of all.* And always remember that *gratitude* expressed prior to the third dimensional realization of the desired outcome is founded in the knowing that *it already exists.* It simply *is!* And all we have to do is *trust* that this is so, which allows us to completely let go, let God…

And allow the Adventures in Manifesting to begin!

About the Author

Dr. Marilyn Joyce, RD, *The Vitality Doctor™, International Radio & Television Personality,* has, for almost 40 years, inspired and transformed hundreds of thousands of lives by educating and entertaining audiences around the globe, both large and small. The *Vibrant Health Guru* to many, Dr. Joyce is an Inspirational Speaker and Trainer, Nutrition and Health Educator, Coach and Consultant.

Her passions in life include speaking on the power of preventive nutrition and lifestyle practices, aging gracefully and agelessly, healthfully and vibrantly, and making complex health and wellness information very user-friendly. She effectively teaches how to conquer your personal energy crisis with quick and easy *Instant E.N.E.R.G.Y.*™ strategies that anyone can do anywhere anytime! Her complimentary e-course and myth busting reports can be found at her websites.

http://www.TransformStressNow.com

http://www.MarilynJoyce.com

THE OPENING OF DOORS

Shawn K. Carpenter

He looked at her, looked into her. Despite the thick fog that seemed to have crept into the furthest recesses of his mind, blanketing any coherent thought, he could still see her. It was her eyes that seemed to plead, "Do this for me. I need you."

She said something to him, but even as she tried to shout over the frenzied roar of the crowd, he was barely able to hear what was said, such was his fear. He had never experienced anything like it. Everything he had done to get ready for this moment had seemed almost excessive at the time. Now he saw just how little it was.

Exhaustion truly was a confidence-killer. Like a deer caught in the headlights, he looked back at his coach. Coach tried to rouse him, tried to encourage him, to push him, to get him back into the fight.

Was it possible to break through the barrier? The barrier that had held him hostage for so long and would continue, with its death-grip, until it nearly cost him everything: his dreams, his home, his marriage, and his kids.

Thankfully, with the grace of the Universe, it didn't end there at the Muay Thai match. If it had, I wouldn't be here writing to you today. You see, for as long as I can remember, there have been pervading forces which seem to be gently (or not so gently) nudging me, helping me to decide the direction of my life.

Primarily, there is a deep longing, a yearning to be who I really am. With that, perhaps even underneath, there has always been an innate awareness: A sense of the reality of that which I seek, a sense of the tremendous potential and gifts I have to share with the world.

I certainly haven't made it easy on myself. This is where another principal force has always acted in direct opposition to that deep-felt yearning: fear.

It seems fear has been there every step of the way, like a nail stuck in your tire that you really only notice when the tire is flat, and forget about as soon as the tire is pumped up again. The fear would sit dormant, like a cobra waiting for a chance to strike, rearing its ugly head whenever I was about to step forward in my life.

Fear of failure, of being hurt, of dying, of living, and of success – Fear in its many guises.

At a very deep level, I have always been committed to the journey – the journey inward to truly living and being all of who I really am. Yet, because of these two continually conflicting forces inside me, this seemingly apparent war, I have never really given an absolute commitment to any one thing – no matter the depth of passion it stirred in me.

In some ways, this very struggle is at the same time a blessing. It is perhaps because of this struggle that I have studied spirituality my entire life. Perhaps it is the reason I also practice the martial arts. Perhaps, it is why I continue to write.

I do know that with any large endeavor in my life, the desire and passion to pursue it has come from a place deep within me, beyond words. During the course of many years teaching, coaching, and mentoring people through martial arts, I have come across the very same passion in many people and quite often, the fear that goes with it…

The fear that ultimately suppresses the passion and keeps people from reaching their potential.

That said, I am glad for all of it, my life I mean; the good and the bad, the beautiful and ugly. My life has been full of ups and downs, full of both triumphs and struggles.

While it is true that everyone encounters the highs and lows of life, in my experience, the people who have truly chosen to pursue their passions will, many times, encounter greater lows, even greater struggles and even greater victories.

While it is easy to say that life is as it should be or that it is all perfect, I would venture to say that life is as it is. This moment is as it 'should' be because it already is as it is. There is no arguing with that fact. Whatever is happening in anyone's life is simply happening. This, of course is based on a lot of factors, not least of which are the choices we make on all levels, hence it is as it 'should' be. But let me back up a bit.

While I have had many incredible experiences, I have also had what I would call many missed opportunities. Why? Because, while it's true that many people simply do their best according to their degree of consciousness, often I simply knew that I could consciously have chosen differently. I had many near successes where I could see and feel how I could have given just a little bit more to achieve the success I desired, and boy have I beaten myself up for it.

Sounds like a bit of a victim story does it not? I know there are many, many people in a similar position. No matter how many books they've read, no matter how many movies they've seen, lectures, seminars and workshops they've attended, no matter how much they've studied the Law of Attraction, living in the present moment, no matter how many prayers and mantras they've said, in their eyes, they've still fallen short, often by only a fraction.

Like many others, I have been blessed with a plethora of knowledge, skills, and talent, much of it stemming from a very clear yearning, and most of it blocked by nearly as big a fear. Yet, that yearning always remained; and still remains to this day. It seems to revolve around five specific areas which became clearer the older (and wiser?) I grew.

Did I ever desire success in those areas? One of those areas, those passions, is writing. Just enough of a shift in my attitude and actions led to the beginning of the fulfillment of a life-long dream. For as long as I can remember, I have dreamed of being a published author. However, it was a dream I had mostly put to the side, partly out of fear, partly due to the demands of daily life, and the pursuit of other dreams.

I have been putting pen to paper all my life, writing sporadically, sometimes feeling more inspired and more capable of pursuing that dream directly. I can remember when my first son was born (he is eleven as I write this), how inspired I was to write as a result of his birth and the experiences we had as a young family. In fact, at the time I even began taking the steps necessary to have my manuscripts published. After taking some serious action, visualizing, etc., I just stopped...

Like so many times prior and so many times since, I quit just shy of the mark.

That's been my experience many times over: a deeper feeling somewhat akin to regret; an entrenched feeling of having just missed, of having come so close to fulfilling my passion but quitting a little too soon.

Why is it that we are passionate about certain things?

It is because passion directs us toward our purpose in life, why we are here, but even more importantly, who we really are. Truth be told, they are inexorably linked.

That is the deep-seated, soulful yearning to which I am referring – not to become more, but to be *who* and *what* we *really* are.

Let's fast-forward to January, 2010. After living a life of almost making it, things were getting worse and worse. Though there were still many happy moments and experiences, there was always an underlying feeling of struggle which would manifest on an external level with ever-increasing frequency.

Remember that I was well aware of the Law of Attraction, how our thoughts create our reality, and how important our vibration is.

Regardless, I couldn't bring myself past negative, depressive and angry states. And those states were affecting everything: my thoughts, words, and actions.

This ultimately led to the dissolution of my business, many family relationships, friendships, and almost my marriage and family life. For as long as I can remember, along with that deep yearning, I have always known there was this one particular woman out there with whom I would spend my entire life, my soul mate, so-to-speak.

A little corny, I know. Here I was, living what could potentially be the life of my dreams, with the love of my life, and I was messing it all up!

That threat of loss provided me with the first of many awakening experiences to come. Though only temporary, I was given a tremendous seeing into the *"is-ness"* of the present moment. So complete was the seeing that I, Shawn K. Carpenter, nearly faded away so all that remained was an ineffable peace. This felt at the same time, both deep inside as at a very still point, and everywhere as an all-encompassing presence.

This presence, or "beingness," if you will, was a confirmation of sorts, a confirmation of that life-long, deep-seated yearning and knowing of which I have been speaking.

At about the same time as this first awakening experience, I had the first of several profound realizations where I was given remarkable insight into my life up to that point, my present circumstances, and where my life was headed if I continued to follow the course I was on. I can remember how the first one nearly took my breath away and stayed with me for several days, like being hit over the head by a two-by-four! It was very humbling, to say the least.

Together, the two types of experiences have given me the strength, inspiration, and determination to take that extra step in pursuing my passions and living a 'life on purpose'.

The idea of alchemy – turning base metal into gold or suffering into consciousness – has always fascinated me, particularly as I see it at work in my own life! For me, it was the threat of serious loss that began the process of enormous change. With that small, but very clear awakening, I was able to make a new commitment. No sooner had I done that, a huge opportunity came my way: I was invited to be part of a writing competition.

Excitedly, I got involved.

Then came the thought, 'Who am I to write about spiritual matters?' And this is where I can say I truly reached a turning point: I didn't let the fear stop me. I had the full support of my beautiful wife.

Did I win the competition? Nope. But I did do really well, moving from over 2500 authors to being part of the last 250. When I was cut, did I quit? Yup. I felt very discouraged but life continued on, now with more intense highs and lows.

Over the course of a year, I came one hair's breath away from losing everything. Only now, the potential loss and the ensuing grief was so incredibly intense that it felt as though my heart were being torn from my chest and ripped in two.

It seemed the Universe was asking me to live up to my commitment, to fulfill my yearning, with a little coercive pressure!

So, I continued writing. I have continued what I began in the contest, putting the finishing touches on my book proposal, with the intent to send it to publishers.

Do I worry, or doubt, or fear? You bet – sometimes, but something has changed. I am now not only okay with the unknown, but I am excited by it. I am not only determined, but very sure of my ability to manifest that which I desire.

Manifesting seems to go hand in hand with the unknown; after all, the unknown is the origin for all that is known, all that is manifested.

Now, I'm sitting here, writing this at Starbucks, and truly conscious of how the pieces of my life are really fitting together. As I have gained the courage to run towards my dreams, I have found that the Universe answers by having my dreams run towards me.

No sooner had I made this new level of commitment that I had some amazing things fall into place, although it required many things to dissolve first. One of those things was my martial arts school that I had run for nine years.

There is definitely something to be said for perseverance. I wholeheartedly believe in the power of commitment. I have learned that part of commitment, especially at such a core level, is the ability to be brutally honest with ourselves, where we are at, and where we would like to be.

Even as one door is closing, I feel that there is something bigger going on. It has become apparent to me that as we align ourselves with our purpose, through our commitment to who we really are, to *beingness*, what could only be called our true desires begin to manifest.

For me, it was one after another: A chance to relocate and explore with my family, an enormous opportunity for my personal martial arts progress, along with a last minute (literally fifteen minutes before our last class) sale of the business.

Truly, as one door closes, others open, we just need to trust the process.

Another of those openings for me is the book you are holding in your hands. When I was part of last year's contest, I had no idea that I would be invited personally, through Facebook, to be part of a compilation book that features best-selling authors, yet here I am. Funny.

About the Author

A dedicated martial artist and spiritual seeker the majority of his life, author Shawn K. Carpenter brings a wealth of experience and knowledge in the areas of martial arts, personal growth, First Nations ceremonies and spiritual development every time he puts pen to paper. Whether he is teaching, involved in ceremony or simply being a father and husband, Shawn continually leads by example, demonstrating the essential balance of a true warrior spirit!

http://www.shawnkcarpenter.ca

FINDING MY TRUTH

Janine Baryza-Ly

We are all connected. We really are all one. It is a scientific fact that we are made of the same matter as the stars and the Universe that surround us.

We are all one.

I need you to know that before I tell you my story and talk about manifestation and consciousness. You need to know that I am connected to you. Whatever you are doing right now is affecting me, and whatever I am doing right now is affecting you. You need to know that, so you are motivated to become what I know you are – love, light, and abundance… so you can support me on my calling, and I can support you in realizing your soul's desire. You may start on your journey for your own gain and personal goals, but as you open up and receive the joy and peace of your own beautiful creations, so will I. And I know that the further your soul opens, my spirit will be given even more freedom to open as well.

I was twenty-four years old, a single mother, and I was mad at the world. I was mad at my recent ex-husband, my family, and just about everyone who told me that life was about struggle. Even more so I was mad at God. I went to church, I followed the rules, I prayed, and yet I still felt as if I was failing at life. The harder I tried to do the right thing, the farther away I became from liking myself.

I was working three different jobs within the same place. I had been promised a promotion that would have set my financial situation at ease, only to have it ripped away at the last second. They just decided to eliminate the position altogether. I remember walking into work every day holding back tears. I couldn't have a breakdown because I needed the work. I wouldn't ask for help from anybody, in the fear that an already broken me would have to hear how broken I really was.

One of my jobs was selling gym memberships. I was selling health and wellness, just about the time that I was the unhealthiest and most unwell. I needed money, and I had no clue how I was going to earn it. So I ran around like a chicken with my head cut off, struggling to make it all work out in an effort to make sure that there would be food on the table. I knew that there had to be a better way to live. I also knew that all the people that had surrounded me at the time didn't know what that better way was. So I gave up.

I sat outside on my front steps and yelled at God. I told him/her that I knew he/she was there, but that I give up. I wasn't going to church anymore or going to try to do the right thing, and that if this everlasting, forgiving God exists, he/she would have to come find me and show me the abundance of what the 'I Am' has promised. I was pissed, and all I asked for was to see truth with a capital 'T'. I didn't even care what that Truth looked like, as long as it was Truth.

I was sick of being lied to. I was sick of society's impressions of good and bad, and I was done with everything fake. I left everything that I was ever taught about life on those front steps. If this is all that life had to offer, then I didn't want to be a part of it. Something had to change.

"Dear God, please come into my whole being and bring me farther than my wildest of dreams, with light and joy." That was, and still is, my prayer.

So there I was; everything that I thought life was about was falling apart. I realized that I wanted a fulfillment that was far beyond anything tangible. I wanted to stop struggling in life, and I wanted to live in joy. I looked up at the sky and demanded that God show me what I knew was inside my heart. I have always been a spiritual person. I have always had the knowingness that there really is a God, the Highest source, the Divine of the Divine. Yet I also realized that the people who taught me about God really missed the mark on what that great energy is in Truth.

Then my life changed. A man with long blond hair tied in a ponytail walked through the doors at the gym. He was inquiring about joining. As we chit chatted a bit, I gave him the usual tour of the place. In actuality, he pissed me off. He asked questions about why our water wasn't filtered because if we were selling health, why wouldn't we have healthy drinking water for our patrons. I remember thinking to myself that he really over-estimated the hearts of men – that all most people want is to make money, not to look out for each other's well-being. Then he said something that I will never forget. Out of the blue, he said, *"Ya know, life is not about doing, it's about not doing"*. I looked at him with a perplexed face and took his business card. Something in my heart told me to listen.

The man with long blond hair happened to be a holistic health practitioner in my neighborhood. It took me about a day, but I called him up to talk. I really wasn't sure what I was calling him for; I just knew that I had to. I knew that he held something different inside of himself, something that no one else around me had…

He spoke Truth, even though I didn't fully understand what that Truth was. He talked about healing.

In order to have everything I have ever imagined and more, I would have to stop what I was doing and realign my life. In order to create something new, I needed to make room for the creation to come in. It was something I had heard before but, until that moment, didn't really believe. In order to do this, I would have to stop. I knew, right then and there, that this was my answer. I was talking to him because somewhere, something heard me, and now I had the choice to accept the opportunity to learn a different way to live. To accept what I was so desperately seeking.

Within two weeks of knowing this man, I quit two of my three jobs, made him hire me, and started to reinvent my life. In order to be where I knew I wanted to be, I had to go beyond the parameters of what I knew. I knew that what I wanted to create was beyond the comprehension of life I was accustomed to, so I had to invite in the unknown to become known.

I don't want you to get the wrong idea. This wasn't easy… If you talk to my mentor, he will probably tell you how much I fought him on his wisdom. However, no matter how much I protested, I knew I had a choice – to keep on doing what was not working in my life, or try a different way. At the end of the day, I saw it was *my* choice. It was up to me to lead me where I wanted to go. He was the first of many who had the understanding that if he helped me, I would be helping him.

So where has this all led me? It has led me right to you, to where you are reading my words. From a nineteen-year-old pregnant girl, to a spiritual Leader and psychic medium, but most of all, to someone who has met God: the real God, Allah, Great Spirit, 'I Am Who Am'. It has led me further than my wildest of dreams, and I still feel as if I am only at the beginning! I can tell you about many amazing stories of miraculous things that have happened since, but in Truth, the most miraculous aspect of this whole journey is that I know that I am loved. No matter what life offers, I know that I am always protected. That is a gift beyond my wildest of dreams.

This journey has led me to an understanding of why we can create our lives. We are loved – truly and unconditionally loved. That love is right there waiting for you to accept it. True love allows you to be who and what you really are. True love accepts and encourages your peace, happiness, joy and most importantly, the wholeness of your spirit. That love that surrounds you is trying to get your attention in every way possible. It is waiting to help you manifest all of your heart's desires. That love knows it will grow stronger the moment you accept it.

From today into eternity, I want you to remember two simple phrases and one simple step that will get you beyond your wildest of dreams:

Say yes! – A manifestation cannot be realized unless you accept the opportunity for it to come into reality. Just having the openness of saying "yes" will manifest opportunities into your life. Even if the opportunity presented isn't exactly what you were looking for, just remember that one thing leads you to the next. You cannot finish a race if you don't take the first step. I see people all the time negate an opportunity because they cannot comprehend the 'how' of the opportunity. It is not up to you to understand 'how' the world works, but to say yes to life, and trust in the process.

Say thank you! – The appreciation and awe of life allow the unknown to open up possibilities that you had never imagined. Release your need to determine whether you are worthy of a gift and just say thank you. Often we talk ourselves out of the miracles in our lives because we don't believe they are meant for us. Here is my trick to life: Believing that everything is a gift is so much more fulfilling than believing that nothing is. I would rather have joy in my life than pain. You are a great gift to this world. Say *thank you.*

Find a support team – To me, this is the most important step. There are many things that you are able to do on your own. However, if you would like to make it easier on yourself, allow others to help you. You are not meant to be alone. We are a part of each other. You cannot have an experience without something or someone to bounce that energy off of. Manifestation does not happen alone; it happens through the collaboration of multiple souls. When you want to manifest light, love and joy, then collaborate with others who are manifesting that energy as well. Make room for the souls who support life and possibilities. Set yourself up for success by surrounding yourself with others who will encourage you on your path – people who will keep you afloat when you want to sink. You may not see them at first, but if you are reading this book, you just introduced yourself to many who believe in your success. Feel that love and accept your greatness.

You are unconditionally loved. Once you accept that you will be led beyond what you can imagine. Love the process and mystery much more than the outcome. Become a part of life. Instead of being an outside observer, be born into creation. Instead of living apart from the creator, see yourself as already whole.

About the Author

Psychic medium Janine Baryza-Ly is a Minister, lecturer, author and licensed Massage Therapist. Most of all she is excited about life! She has the ability to communicate with loved ones, angels, guides and energies in the beyond under God. It is her soul's passion, to share, teach, learn and experience the limitless possibilities and miracles that God truly has to offer.

Author of the book *'Intuition, a Spiritual Yet Practice Guide'*, Janine shows her devotion to enlighten everyone to their own gifts and abilities. *'I AM The Beyond'* is her latest book. This children's book expresses the most important message she has ever known; you are never alone, you are always guided and you are loved. This is a message for all religions, spiritual traditions and ages.

Co-owner of 'The Beyond Center', Janine and her partner Rebecca Anne Locicero have devoted themselves to enlightening community as a whole through God, Divine Intuition, Awareness and Love.

http://www.AQuestForTruth.com

http://www.TheBeyondCenter.com

THE PUZZLE OF LIFE

Jonathan Yudis

Have you ever put together a jigsaw puzzle? Imagine for a moment that each of us is a completely unique puzzle, and that manifesting our dreams is simply a matter of putting together the puzzle pieces of our life. First, we must recognize that our lives are made up of thousands, if not millions, of different fragmented components and living parts. Separated and on their own, they might not look like much, but once they are synthesized and inter-connected, an awesome and beautiful mosaic manifests before us. This is the tapestry of our life and the key to us accessing our true-life purpose.

Getting Started

Before we are able to begin the conscious process of connecting our puzzle, we must have a reason for doing so. As the saying goes, if we do not know the *'why'*, we cannot know the *'how'* in terms of manifesting our dreams. In the classic tale of Siddhartha, the Buddha, it is only after he learns that the world is full of pain and suffering that he longs to be enlightened and free. In my case, it was only after weathering challenges and living in prolonged stress that I found the impetus to manifest profound change in my life.

Creating the Picture

As humans, we have been given the ultimate gift of free choice and live in an ever-evolving Universe, which means we get to choose or create the picture of what we want our lives to look like. If we find that our lives still seem to be in various disconnected pieces, it is often because we've lost sight of this picture.

Visioning is an amazing opportunity to synthesize everything together into a unified whole. Once we create such a vision, we know what our puzzle is supposed to look like. Then, we can begin to put it together, one piece at a time. While this might sound like a daunting task, it's actually the growth process itself, and we've been doing it our whole lives.

Fiction vs. Reality

We must ask, "What is the current state of my personal puzzle?" Figuring this out involves taking an honest inventory of our lives exactly as they are in this moment. When I did this, I discovered that there was an enormous gap between the *fiction* of my life and the *reality* of how I was experiencing it. In general, the *fiction* of our lives is how things appear to be on the surface, while the *reality* is how they are truly unfolding within us.

Here are some of the details from the *fiction* of my life:

- *Tag Line*: I was living the dream.

- *Family & Home*: I had an amazing wife, beautiful children, and great friends. We lived in a nice (nearly million dollar) home in a highly sought after suburban neighborhood of Los Angeles, California where my kids went to an award-winning public school.

- *Work & Career*: I worked in the entertainment industry. I was a heartbeat away from Hollywood and every major film studio and in the perfect place for career opportunities.

- *Finance & Lifestyle*: The bills are all getting paid. We have nice cars and enjoy an active lifestyle.

- Here are some of the details from the *reality* of my life:

- *Tag Line*: I'm living out of synch with myself.

- *Family & Home*: While my family and their love are the best parts of my life, my time with them is often stressed and compromised because of my constant efforts to improve career and finances. While I've always dreamed of living in a home on a quiet street, ours is very busy (and potentially dangerous for the kids) with cars constantly passing by.

- *Work & Career*: No matter how hard I work, I never seem to get 'in' the proverbial door of the entertainment industry. I spend more of my time stressing to get work than working.

- *Finance & Lifestyle*: No matter how much money I earn, it's never enough. In an effort to keep everything going, I find myself going deeper and deeper into financial debt. The more debt I incur, the more desperate I become to 'make it' and alleviate our situation. While our life might appear great on the surface, our lifestyle is unsustainable and stressful, and therefore unfulfilling.

In my personal case, part of my *fiction* was that 'everything is great' when in fact, this was not true. Since I knew it was time to re-envision my life puzzle, I created a dynamic 'vision board' filled with words and images of everything I committed to manifesting in my life.

Letting Go

After creating my vision board, the next big step I took was 'letting go.' Letting go or surrendering is perhaps the ultimate action we can take in transforming our lives.

However, there is a huge difference between *letting go* and *giving up*. Letting go refers to allowing what already is to be, while giving up refers to no longer making an effort to persevere through life's countless challenges.

I recently saw my son struggling with a toy, which illustrates the difference. He was playing with a cylindrical finger trap where his index fingers got inserted, and then as he pulled to release them, the webbing of the toy tightened around his fingers. The more he struggled and pulled, the more stuck his fingers became. Even though he kept saying, "I give up," he continued to struggle with the finger trap. Finally I said, "Just relax and let go," and he stopped struggling. As soon as he let go of struggling with his fingers, the webbing loosened up and he was easily able to release them. While this example might seem like a cliché, it's how we are often dealing with the most serious challenges in our lives.

For me, letting go meant accepting that the specific outcomes I'd been working towards for so long were not going to happen. What made this 'letting go' process so difficult was that for years, I had focused on all of my previous efforts. Once I finally just *let go,* something truly unexpected occurred – the borders around the frame of my perspective disappeared. I was finally able to understand what I had been after all along.

We think we want *things,* but what we truly want is *states of being.* For example, I thought I wanted fame, but what I was after was the opportunities I believed fame offered like being able to influence and inspire others, which is very possible even without fame. Ironically, this letting go process does not actually mean that these original outcomes cannot come to pass, but rather that we must not limit ourselves in pre-defining the ways in which they manifest.

Synchronize

Each of us has our own unique rhythm or timing in the way we live our lives. It is essential that we know our own timing in life and become in synch with it. As we grow, we change, and if we remain open to it instead of resisting such change, we stay in synch with ourselves. If we do not, we fall out of synch, and the structure we have built for our life puzzle begins to fall apart.

In many ways, we are like plants – if we are not growing, we are dying. Sometimes this growth requires growing pains, but these are necessary so that we can blossom into our fullest potential. To synchronize means to cause or operate at the same time. In order to be happy and manifest our dreams, we must be in synch with ourselves!

Environment

In terms of how I really created massive change, first came the internal work such as taking personal inventory and responsibility for all the scattered pieces of my life and then letting go and visioning a new reality. As a result of this internal work, everything changed externally as well. My biggest change resulted from a decision to switch living environments.

I realized that while I have always felt optimal vitality while immersed in nature, I had been living in urban environments for nearly 15 years. Since I knew I had become out of synch with myself, I began to seriously consider moving to an environment where nature was a dominant force and inspiration. This decision also meant that I was open to living in an environment that supported my present priorities instead of those that had become outdated. Instead of living somewhere because it was supposed to help my career, I chose to live somewhere I was truly inspired, knowing that this inspiration could only serve my career as well.

Faith

The final ingredient in putting all the pieces of my life puzzle together was, and definitely is, faith. Faith represents that unexplainable inner knowing that regardless of appearances or even how we feel, everything is as it should be and will work out perfectly. Now more than ever, we all need to find and cultivate faith in our lives and in ourselves.

It is very difficult to see the big picture of our dreams manifesting on a daily basis. If one were driving from New York to Los Angeles and looking down at the road every ten feet, they would most likely become discouraged after seeing many miles of similar looking pavement. Only faith that we are indeed driving in the right direction will allow us to keep going and ultimately reach our desired destination. Faith also empowers us to stay the course when we recognize we have taken a detour or even gotten lost along the way.

I've always loved the phrase, *"Life is a journey, not a destination."* Since we're all on this magical journey of manifestation, remember to celebrate your wins and help others do so along the way. Over the course of our lives, we might only manifest a few massive milestones like graduating from high school or college, getting married or finding someone we truly love, the birth of a child, or a great creative success or career accomplishment. These huge milestones are actually the results of countless smaller 'wins' that occur in our lives daily. The more we recognize and acknowledge all of our wins, the more we validate and empower ourselves to create greater ones. These 'wins' might seem insignificant, but they add up to become who we are and what we are manifesting.

Discovering the Hologram in the Puzzle

Getting back to the puzzle, there is something extraordinary that I discovered along the way. Have you ever seen those holographic image books with pages of pictures and designs that just look like blobs of shapes and colors? They don't make any sense until you stare at them in a completely relaxed way. Then, out of nowhere an incredible holographic picture emerges. This is what happens when we commit to manifesting our dreams and synthesizing our life puzzle. No matter what you imagine or put together on a vision board, the picture is still two-dimensional. Once you commit to making it happen and start taking decisive actions, another image reveals itself – the hologram within the puzzle. This hologram is the hidden treasure, the writing between the lines, or our true purpose behind the visible appearance of our lives.

As a direct result of letting go of outdated expectations and taking full responsibility for my life exactly as it is, I have successfully reconnected my life puzzle and I am manifesting my greatest dreams. I presently live in an environment which humbles, sustains, and inspires me. I live in a new home on a quiet street where my family continues to grow and thrive. Most importantly, I am living in synch with myself, more and more in the moment, which allows me to express the love and gratitude that envelop me.

None of us knows how long we will be here or how many tomorrows we will have. All we are guaranteed is today, this moment. So let us manifest our dreams today and celebrate them always!

About the Author

Jonathan Yudis is an award winning filmmaker, motivational author and speaker, and Yogi Siromani.

He graduated Suma Cum Laude from New York University with a BFA in Film and Television, and holds an MFA from the directing discipline at the American Film Institute. He actively writes, produces, and directs feature films, television, and live theatrical events. Some of his credits include Walt

Disney's POCAHONTAS II (rotoscoping), the media campaign for 'P:5Y – PEACE IN 5 YEARS' and the film 'CHRIST IN GETHSEMANE,' both of which received Telly awards in 2010 & 2011.

He is president and creative director at 'INFINITE ENTERTAINMENT NOW,' a visionary media company. Current projects include: the book and seminar: 'THE DIVINE SYNTHESIS: Living Right Now,' developing an International Spiritual Congress to be held on 12-21-12, and the feature films: 'YOGI' based on the life of Paramhansa Yogananda', and 'THE LOST YEARS', based on the life of Jesus.

Since 1993, Jonathan has led motivational classes, workshops and seminars on yoga, film, and spirituality to thousands of participants throughout the United States. He enjoys time immersed in nature and lives with an ongoing attitude of gratitude on the island of Maui with his wife and children.

http://www.JonathanYudis.com

CREATING GREATNESS
FOR THE GREATER GOOD

Michael Cheng

This is a story of how, in June 2011, I manifested one of my many childhood dreams. I share it with you in the hope that it will inspire a paradigm shift in your mind that will change your life forever!

"In October 1996, I awakened in the hospital from an eight-day long medically induced coma with a broken neck, eleven fractured ribs, a fractured pelvis, a lung contusion, and a damaged kidney. My lip had to be sewn back on to my face, and to make matters worse, doctors did not detect my cervical spine (odontoid) fracture until six months had passed.

Following a flight to Germany to undergo an imminent corrective spinal operation and excruciating rehabilitation process, I was placed in a halo jacket, screwed to my cranium with four bolts. After a summer of looking like Frankenstein and wearing the contraption had passed, I revisited Germany for a second operation.

To this day it is not fully clear what actually caused the auto-collision – it will however remain forever in my memory as a fateful event that permanently changed my view of life.

Fortunately, I have discovered that there are rewards for being able to withstand agony. The *emotional* and physical pain that I endured taught me an important lesson: what does not kill me makes me stronger.

A challenge faced, whether or not it is overcome, still promotes growth.

After achieving a nearly perfect recovery from such severe injuries, I know I can confront any obstacle that challenges me. Conquering such a trial is an accomplishment that I constantly use to motivate myself, as well as others.

I have survived and conquered what seemed to be unconquerable, and I have been given a second chance to live. With this second chance, I have been able to *initiate an exciting vision for my future. I dare to dream big dreams, and I dream of becoming an inspiration on a large scale to those who can benefit from it."*

The passage above is an excerpt from my college application essay, which I wrote in 1997 when I was sixteen years old. Back then, I didn't know what the 'Natural Law of Attraction' was, but apparently I was already dreaming and envisioning a future that I would one day manifest.

Fourteen years after I dreamed of becoming an 'inspiration,' I was presented with the opportunity to inspire others by having my story (this chapter) published right alongside the writings of one of my favorite personal development experts, Brian Tracy. I can honestly say that I've developed the majority of my business philosophies, success strategies, and practices as a result of studying the ideas of Brian Tracy.

The publishing of this particular chapter is actually the manifestation of a dream I envisioned on the New Year's Eve of 2008. Back then, while I was brainstorming, recollecting, dreaming, making plans, and writing down my goals for the future, I remember thinking, "How cool would it be to become a writer some day and become an inspiring author like Brian Tracy, Tony Robbins, John Assaraf, Wayne Dyer and some of my other favorite inspirational mentors? I want to one day become one of the few Chinese-American personal development experts and inspirational speakers. How I am going to accomplish this, I have no idea, but now that I know I want it, I know it must happen."

There has been a lot of controversy and debate regarding the efficacy of the Natural Law of Attraction. I am no expert when it comes to using it to manifest goals and dreams. Nor do I consider myself an expert in inspiration or personal development. In fact, I must admit that I was once one of those skeptics who doubted the validity of the Law of Attraction – that is until I learned from Dr. Wayne Dyer the reason why manifesting can only be real – a theory I will elaborate on later.

48

Ever since I started believing in the Law of Attraction, my life has improved dramatically and become more abundant. Now I am a firm believer and successful practitioner of this ritual some have called 'The Secret.'

The fact that you are reading this chapter is proof that my dreams and visions are manifesting, and therefore, anyone can manifest as long as they have the belief they can.

To my knowledge, there are some specific ways manifesting happens, as well as some other philosophies I've learned that can make it even easier to manifest.

The steps to follow are that you must ...

- *Know specifically what you want* – vagueness is the adversary of the Law of Attraction. The more clearly you can envision what you desire, the quicker your path will be to getting there.

- *Know who you are and what you want in your life* – you must have clearly defined goals.

- *Fully believe* that what you want to manifest is truly what you want.

- *Be confident* that you deserve that which you wish to manifest.

- *Be patient and have faith* that your dreams will manifest over time. Some manifestations happen instantly, others take years.

Manifesting isn't at all difficult. The hardest part is really the first part: really knowing what you want and believing you deserve it.

How did I discover what I wanted?

One of my heroines is philanthropist Karen Tse, who once said, *"When you sit within the silence of your soul, you know where to go. You know where to lead."*

To me, following this advice was the most critical step in manifesting. You must take the time to sit in the silence of your soul and ask yourself what you want.

Any person who has manifested will tell you that if you want to manifest desires born from vengeful, selfish, greedy, or other negative thoughts, you will never be able to manifest them.

How then do you know if what you want is not selfish or negative?

Dr. Wayne Dyer says:

"There is no greater power in heaven or on earth than pure, unconditional love. In your quiet time, think about only peace and love. What can you expect as you practice a few days of total unconditional love? Your thought forms of unconditional love will *begin to produce what you desire without your even being aware of how it is happening. Your dreams will be more intense, and the vision of your purpose will become clearer.*"

I draw my confidence in knowing that I deserve what I desire because I have decided that it is my obligation and my purpose to serve the world to make it a better place. I have witnessed that life becomes beautiful and meaningful when you decide to harness unconditional love for others. This unconditional love forms the foundation for all my intentions, desires, and manifestations; it makes my life much easier and fills it with abundance. This is why I have been able to confidently manifest many things that I have wanted.

Good things happen to those who love the world around them. You always have the choice whether or not you want to unconditionally love the world. Like Dr. Dyer says, why don't you practice it for a few days, and see for yourself what ends up happening?

In my journey of self-discovery over the last fifteen years, I have taken time out daily for soul-searching. When I soul-search, I look to fully discover who I am, why I live, and how I will serve the world. When I ask myself who I am, part of the answer is a first-generation Taiwanese-American, with a calling from my inner source. It reminds me that I am on a mission with a special purpose.

I was not born just to get rich, enjoy life, or see that my family and friends are happy. I was not born so I could just enjoy freedom. My journey of self-discovery has led me to envision a life of diligence, sacrifice, and benevolence.

I've realized that I was born an American so I could learn how to think like one. While I recognize that my ancestors are from China, I question why I was born into a life of liberty and awareness, while a billion neglected and uneducated rural poverty-stricken Chinese are born into lives of global ignorance. With this perspective, I am compelled to feel even more unconditional love for all the less fortunate people around the world.

These feelings have led me to become an entrepreneur in the real estate development and education fields. I chose the 'road less traveled' of being a spiritual, altruistic entrepreneur because it is highly rewarding. The most important reward that has come from being an entrepreneur is not financial, but the opportunity to practice the qualities of a philanthropic leader. As Confucius said, "He who would be master must be servant of all."

As an entrepreneur with unconditional love, who has the power to manifest goodness, it breaks my heart to witness the social inequalities and disharmony in our world. I would feel ashamed if I was still trying to manifest the 'American Dream' without the underlying desire to make the world a better place. If I could say that there was a secret behind 'The Secret', then it is wishing for things that can improve you, so you have more power, wisdom, and resources to make the world a better place.

With a loving challenge to you, I'll end on this note:

Dare to be more, do more, and have more. Bless the ones you love by exposing them to your true inescapable identity. You owe it to yourself and this world to become the person you were born to be by shedding any skepticism or cynicism that detains you on your path to becoming courageous and fearless. Amplify reality as you know it by obeying the voice within you. Make your mark, enlighten others, and redefine what it really means to *live*.

Your thoughts and choices will reshape your destiny. If you have not yet figured out what it is you want, then now is the time to free your mind and dare to dream. Dream about things you want and deserve to have, and make sure you dream big. Never forget, dreaming big without working hard, makes you a megalomaniac! Make haste and make your move, because, as my brother Alan taught me, "Success waits for nobody!"

About the Author

Michael Cheng is a multilingual, American internet entrepreneur and real estate developer. He is the founder and President of 'Mando Mandarin', the online school which specializes in teaching Chinese as a foreign language using a distance-learning approach. He is a pioneering American educator who has connected schools and students around the world to teachers who are physically located in China (www.mandomandarin.com).

He is also the founder of 'Epos Global Management', a New York based real estate development and property management company. Mike donates his time and money to his 'Pencils of Promise' and Wokai.org.

Mike graduated from the Stern School of Business at NYU with a B.S. in Marketing, and is an expert in real estate finance, sales copywriting, and business development. His work has been featured in the New York Daily News, NY1 TV News Channel, and the Chinese World Journal newspaper.

He currently lives in Flushing, NY where he has an interest in politics and aspires to become a community leader.

He regularly travels between New York and Shanghai, while building a Sino-American business network. He believes the world needs more unofficial ambassadors of socio-cultural exchange between nations -- those who can build bridges of peace and eradicate barriers to understanding: "When there is understanding between people, there is less room for fear and a much higher chance for positive synergy and progress." His hobbies are hanging out with his bearded-collie Duke, traveling, learning foreign languages, martial arts, and basketball.

http://www.mandomandarin.com

WHAT'S LUCK GOT TO DO WITH IT?

Fred Alan Wolf

Ever wonder how lucky or unlucky you are? Or, do you think that whatever success or failure you've had, had nothing to do with luck at all? Well if the quantum world of atoms, molecules, and subatomic particles has anything to do with it, not a single moment has passed by without lady luck looking over your shoulder as you attempted to draw to that inside straight called the game of life. Yet there is way to beat lady luck at her game. All you need to do is look at the world vigilantly and carefully enough.

Quantum physics is the theory of the behavior of matter and energy, particularly at the level of atoms and subatomic particles. It is nearly impossible to imagine the strangeness of the behavior of matter at this level. An electron in an atom, for example, performs a trick much like the crew aboard the Enterprise in the well-known Star Trek series, when it "beams" from one energy level to another. It simply jumps from one place to another without going in between. But if we aren't watching it jump, we have no control as to when it will happen.

But suppose we do watch? Then the bizarre world of quantum physics enters our modern lives. Based on the mathematical laws of probability, quantum physics doesn't ordinarily allow us to make predictions that we can trust. Hence one might believe that nothing could be determined and that success and failure were mere whims of chance. However, it turns out that if current experiments in quantum physics are relevant to our everyday experiences and we can learn to observe our lives carefully, and vigilantly enough, we can actually alter the crapshoot of life. But, there is a catch to all this; you need to begin to see things quantum mechanically.

The quantum physical worldview is very different from the world we ordinarily see. However the difference is slight in everyday life. According to quantum physics, there is no reality until that reality is perceived. We call this "the observer effect." Because we usually don't pay attention to ourselves in the perception process, our immediate experience will usually not appear to show how our actions of perception changed anything. However, if we construct a careful history of our perceptions they often show us that our way of perceiving indeed changed the course of our personal history.

That may make sense to you when looking at something new and deciding what it means. But you may wonder, "I'm not actually changing reality, am I? I'm just changing my interpretation of reality." The answer is often difficult to appreciate, but as surprising as it may seem, you are changing reality simply by observing it. In the world described successfully by quantum mechanics, ultimately and fundamentally observers affect the universe whenever they observe it or anything in it. If we refine our ability to see by looking at atomic and subatomic processes the differences would be quite magnified and astonishing to our normal way of seeing.

How do you change your way of seeing? I wish to consider your will here, specifically how it manifests in the physical world. Consider: how is it that what you wish to accomplish sometimes occurs without seeming effort, while at other times, even with great expenditure of energy, you fail in your endeavors? According to the quantum physics way of seeing, observation and awareness tie your mind to the physical world through your desire and that desire manifests as a physical force.

Desire first appears in the mind as a mental formation—the object of desire. When this form manifests, desire holds or preserves it in mind. The power to hold the image, determined by the time-span the image is held, is called intent. Next the object that appeals to your senses is sought for in the physical world if it is not present, and mind-object and the physical object are brought together and superimposed in the mind-space in much the same way you fuse two two-dimensional images together, making one three-dimensional image when you look at an object using your two eyes.

Desire, through your vigilance of observation, actually modifies and alters the course of the physical world, particularly your course through it, causing things to occur that would not normally occur if they were not desired. All of this makes up what shamans call Intent.

Intent operates in the physical world by altering the observed state of that world. Quantum physicists, Yakir Aharonov and M. Vardi discovered that intent affects the physical world. They showed that the old proverb "a watched pot never boils" might have a range of validity previously unsuspected when they discovered the paradoxical situation that arises when a quantum system is watched carefully. If it is monitored vigilantly, it will do practically anything. Imagine a tiny quantum-sized pot of water being heated on a really tiny stove. We all know pots of water boil, given a few minutes or so. You would certainly think the watched quantum pot would also boil. It turns out, because of vigilant observations, the boiling never occurs; the watched quantum pot never boils. All vigilantly watched "quantum pots" never boil, even if they are heated forever.

All of this might be considered just quantum physical speculation. However, in 1989, physicist Wayne Itano and his colleagues at the National Institute of Standards and Technology in Boulder, Colorado experimentally observed the equivalent of the "quantum watched pot" and, indeed, it never boiled! Their experiment involved watching some five thousand beryllium atoms confined in a magnetic field and then exposed to radio waves of energy. The atoms were the equals of quantum pots of water and the radio waves the equivalent of the heat applied to the pot. Under such circumstances the atoms will "evolve" into excited atomic energy states as they absorb the radio energy. Nearly all five thousand will reach their excited state-goals in a little over two hundred fifty milliseconds, that is, a quarter of a second.

To check this, the physicists would observe the atoms after a quarter of a second by shining a short pulse of laser light into their midst. Hot (excited) atoms do not absorb and immediately reemit the laser energy. Atoms that remained cool (in the unexcited state) do. So, by observing the scattered laser light after it passed through the trapped atoms, the physicists were able to determine just how many atoms were hot.

Virtually none were after two hundred fifty milliseconds. We could refer to this as the unwatched pot that naturally evolved to the boiling state in a quarter of a second. But then the scientists became slightly vigilant. They decided to look at the atoms halfway along, after 125 milliseconds (an eighth of second) had passed. So an eighth of second after starting the experiment the laser pulse was turned on and then, at the two hundred fifty millisecond mark the scientist looked again and found that only one-half of the atoms were hot. They repeated the experiment by looking in at 62.5 milliseconds, 125 milliseconds, 187.5 milliseconds, and two hundred fifty milliseconds; in other words, they divided the one-quarter second interval into four equal parts. They were surprised to find that their enhanced vigilance resulted in only one-third of the atoms boiled by the end of the complete period of two hundred fifty milliseconds.

Next they redoubled their vigilance by looking in 16 times, 32 times and finally 64 times during the two hundred fifty milliseconds interval. In the final experiment where they watched their tiny atomic "pots" in 64 equally spaced tiny time intervals, virtually none of the atoms were ever found in an excited state, even though two hundred fifty milliseconds had passed. They all remained frozen in their ground or original states just as they were when the experiment began. In each experiment, mind you, the "heat" was on—the radio waves were continuously sent into the magnetically trapped beryllium atoms.

This implies there is a deep connection between the observer and the observed. So deep, in fact, that we really cannot separate them. All we can do is alter the way we experience reality. This is where intent comes in.

If a system were unobserved, it would certainly undergo the natural physical transition. The pot would boil. The observer effect causes the anomaly to occur. When the system is first observed, it is seen to be in its initial state. When it is observed just a smidgen of time later, well before the time in which it should change, the system is observed with more than 99.99 percent chance to be in its initial state. Like resetting a stop-clock, this flips the odds from 99.99 percent to 100 percent. In other words, the system is found to be exactly where it was initially. Now repeat this measurement again and again, each time just a tiny bit of time later, and with a very high probability, the same observation occurs: The system is found in its initial state

As time marches on, and eventually we pass all reasonable time limits for the transition to occur; it still doesn't happen. The system "freezes" in its initial state. The only requirement to freeze the motion is that the observer must have the intent to see the object in its initial state when he looks. This intent is determined by the frequency of his observations. He must look and find the object in the same state repeatedly in very short time intervals. Eventually a longer period of time passes

We might question the physicists as to their mental intent on doing the experiment. We don't have to. By observing the system as they did, their intent was already established, already "out there," regardless of what they were actually thinking at that time. In other words, their intent was already a physical manifestation determined by the frequency of their observations. The old adage with a twist: you will see it when you believe it.

Suppose a physicist doesn't watch vigilantly or suppose that she or he does but with the intent of seeing it evolve naturally. Then what? Take the quantum pot. If the physicist looks intermittently, expecting it to boil eventually, the pot will follow its natural unobserved course and will boil as proved. These observations, because they are infrequent, have little effect on the natural result. Or if the physicist wishes, she or he may observe the object vigilantly along its natural evolution, and will observe the same result. In other words, a watched pot boils if you intend it to.

Finally, there is another bizarre element to this. Suppose the system could be observed to evolve along a bizarre path, a highly improbable mission, so to speak. If the intent to observe that occurrence is vigilant enough, the object will actually follow the bizarre path of evolution. You can make things happen simply by intending them to happen if you observe with great vigilance—intense observation occurring over very short time intervals—more or less continuously but along a new, unexpected track.

I need to caution the reader here. The bizarre path of evolution seems strange because it violates the second law of thermodynamics. It seems to move energy from a cold to a hot body without performing any work. Although such a path of evolution does not violate the law of conservation of energy and, therefore, is possible, it certainly is not very probable. However, this is no problem in quantum physics: Even the most improbable occurs once in a while. The observer here is vigilantly watching for that rare occurrence and ignoring the usual by not even looking for the normal path of evolution. Hence a watched pot boils on a cake of ice, if you intend it to.

I need to point out that intent and intentions are not the same. Intent refers to a vigorous action of vigilant observations along a specific path of evolution. It matters little what you hope for or even what you passively expect will happen. You need to actively pursue your vision to manifest intent in the physical world, not passively dream about it and hope it will come true. The direction of evolution is determined as you go and depends on where you focus your observation. Thus, intent requires a quantum physical basis. Intention, on the other hand, is a classical mechanical concept. One sets in motion a certain expectation and then hopes for the best. The old adage "the best laid plans of mice and men often go astray" tells the whole story.

Our brains may be composed of like quantum systems, and consequently our paths through history may be governed by the "pot-watched-with-intent" theory. Thus, this may be how will and intent actually govern the movement of living sentient systems.

Luck has nothing to do with it.

About the Author

Fred Alan Wolf is the National Book Award-winning author of *Taking the Quantum Leap*, *The Spiritual Universe* and 13 other books and 3 audio books. His latest book is entitled *Time-loops and Space-twists: How God Created the Universe*. He has appeared in a number of films including: 'THE SECRET' and 'What The Bleep Do We Know?'

Dr. Fred Alan Wolf aka Dr. Quantum earned a Ph. D. in theoretical physics from UCLA. He continues to write, lecture throughout the world, and conduct research on the relationship of quantum physics to consciousness. He is the National Book Award Winning author of *Taking the Quantum Leap* and many other books including *Mind into Matter* and *The Yoga of Time Travel*. He is a member of the Martin Luther King, Jr. Collegium of Scholars. Dr. Wolf has taught at the University of London, the University of Paris, the Hahn-Meitner Institute for Nuclear Physics in Berlin, The Hebrew University of Jerusalem, and San Diego State University in the United States and has been featured in internationally released films and television shows.

http://www.fredalanwolf.com

NOTHING IS BEYOND YOUR REACH

Angelica Irizarry

My love for distant lands all started when I was a little girl. I don't know who or what triggered it, but one day I woke up and realized that I loved the whole world and everyone in it. I wanted to let each and every person in the world know that personally. I suppose that is why I spent most of my life trying to understand and break cultural barriers by learning as much about the world as I possibly could.

As a child I would sit out of games to play pretend, imagining myself in faraway places, braving sand storms and having tea with a maharaja. Every night I would put myself to sleep with some fantastical tale of me traveling to other nations just like Indiana Jones and having adventures. Once I learned how to read, my disposition only grew to more expanded horizons. I would read stories of foreign heroes and heroines of eras past and I would become a part of their worlds. I felt one with them and wanted to find them and let them know how much I loved them. These stories inspired me to believe in the impossible and it was then that I formed the question that would be the driving force behind all of my actions forever after: can life be like a fairytale? It wouldn't be until I was twenty years old that I would begin to imagine the possibility of me actually writing my own fairy tale by travelling to the other side of the earth and fulfilling my dreams.

By the time I started college however, travel was starting to look like something I would do in the distant future, perhaps during my retirement. Money was tight and I was attending school with the help of financial aid. Focusing on college forced me to put my love for travel in the background indefinitely. By then, I had discovered two new passions, acting and dancing. I was working hard to eventually be able to make money in these fields. Since the university I was attending was primarily a business school, I was having difficulty aligning it with my artistic personality and was advised to go to a school that specialized in the field of performing arts.

So I searched the vast majority of performing arts colleges until I came upon a seemingly perfect school. From the classrooms to the courses it appeared to be everything I would ever want in a school. To top it all off, it was an accredited school so all of my previous credits would transfer without a hassle. It was truly a performing artist's dream.

So I couldn't understand why, when I found it, instead of being immensely elated I felt strangely conflicted instead. The more I thought about going the more conflicted I became. I thought that time would eventually carry the expected excitement, but as the days passed my confusion worsened. I didn't understand why but I felt trapped, as if I was drifting further away from what I wanted. The need to make a decision became so stressful that I couldn't function. My mind felt like a dense cloud of black smoke and my body was weak as if recovering from a sickness.

In this state I gave up on trying to make a decision. I lay empty and silent, staring blankly into nothingness and listening to the silence. Suddenly I was taken by the urge to color. I got paper and crayon, turned some music on, and for an hour and a half colored vigorously as if my inner child had woken up from a deep sleep. When I finished I had colored on four pieces of paper. When I looked at the papers I saw my heart's desire staring back.

The words 'travel', 'adventure', and 'follow your joy', were written on them along with a picture of me on a boat with the wind in my hair. One sheet of paper was divided in half with my master plan of two years of school, then job, then family on one side, and the word adventure on the other. While the 'adventure' side was blank except for an erratic scribble underneath the word, the 'master plan' side was densely colored in and organized. I had crossed it out. Landing on me like a storm blown house from Kansas my dreams came rushing back from my childhood. I knew what I had to do.

That night I told my mother the verdict: I wanted to postpone my education indefinitely to travel the world. I explained how I had the travel bug for ten years and how it came back to bite me right at the moment that I needed it. Surprisingly, she thought that it was a good idea and jumped right on the bandwagon volunteering to come with me, reminding me why she was also my best friend. We zoned in on the last country I discovered before I started college and chose India as our destination. And so it happened that with two years of college under my belt I was going to travel the world and educate myself with real life experiences, making the dream of my childhood a reality.

I could feel it, I could even see it. When I closed my eyes and envisioned the future I could see the future me smiling and waving back, promising me that I was headed in the right direction. It was all so real; I knew that my dreams were tangible and that they were right within my grasp. Yet, I was finding it difficult not to sabotage them with my thoughts and worries. No matter what I did I couldn't stop the worries. I kept thinking thoughts like "What if I don't make it?", "I'm too poor, nobody gets it that easy", "What makes me think I'm so special", and "I'm going to suffer for being so lazy".

I realized that all of these thoughts started coming because I had decided to leave the one place that was sending me secure cash flow: school. I knew in my heart that money was not a good reason to stay anywhere, and I was proud that I was not willing to sacrifice my joy for security. Yet I still could not shake the conditions that I needed money to follow my joy. It was true that whenever I closed my eyes, I was there in the future, smiling and waving with everything my heart ever desired, but I had no idea how I was going to get there. It was like trying to look through a cloud of dense fog and it scared me.

I needed a sign to let me know I was on the right path. I looked and waited with bated breath for something that would clearly inform me I was doing the right thing. Like a message on a license plate or a sign on a store window. I waited and searched, begged and pleaded for a sign, and waited for the okay to go and fulfill my crazy dreams. However, nothing came. In fact, more obstacles than doorways seemed to be opening.

Every time I attempted to look in the travel section at the bookstore, someone was in my way. Every time I got extra money, something important came up where I had to spend it. I was getting more and more discouraged when suddenly my mom became unemployed and all of our plans seemed to halt.

I wanted to blame everything on some evil force that was trying to stop me, but I knew that it was me who was sabotaging my own manifestation. Then one day my mom said something that changed everything. She told me that the fact I felt joy in my heart to travel was the sign from the Universe to follow my dreams. I didn't need a piano to fall from the sky to affirm my beliefs. Something as subtle as the feeling of something pulling at my heart strings was proof enough that I was on the right path

I realized then that it was my attachment that was sabotaging my manifestation. My fear and need for a sign were blocking my ability to create and the obstacles were a result of that fear. They were there to teach me an important lesson in manifestation: never take no for an answer. Instead of using them as a sign to forget my dreams, I should have believed in them undoubtedly and used that belief to give me the strength to try until I won my prize.

After this realization I started seeing signs everywhere, in things I had never paid attention to before; in nature, overheard conversations, small coincidences and accidents of time. I used this newfound strength to approach my manifestation with full force. I found pictures, clippings, and names of places I had liked years ago. I used them to conduct searches online about what I thought I wanted to do in India.

I came upon an acting school in India that was owned by a prominent actor there. Like a bride finding the perfect wedding dress, I cried and knew in my heart that this was the one. Later on, it was suggested to me that I go to 'Amma's Yoga Center'. All of the pieces to the puzzle were starting to come together. My mother and I spoke to the necessary people and knocked down doors when we had to. Down to nearly our last dollar, money suddenly started coming in all directions and soon we were able to save enough to go on our trip. I was starting to believe again that life could be like a fairy tale.

In less than a year our lives went from struggling to maintain a normal life, in near poverty, to fulfilling our dreams and travelling the world. Sometime after the previous events, my mother and I decided to add another country to our itinerary. By the time you are reading this we will either be in England sipping tea or in India meditating. I feel I have grown more in one year than I had in the previous five.

Like scouring my feverish imagination as a child, I realized that nothing was beyond my reach when I closed my eyes and made possible the impossible.

If anyone asked me how to find your joy, my advice is simple. The way to finding your joy and fulfilling your dreams is through a child's eyes. Anything is possible to a child, and the road to happiness can sometimes be only one finger painting away. I would also say that when trying to manifest, do not expect the answer to fall into your hands. You have to go looking for it, and fight for it. If you believe in it with all of your heart, and no matter what your reality looks like, you cannot be afraid of not receiving it. You have to know and feel it will happen. I suppose that when the Universe sees you do all you can for your joy, never giving up on it, while at the same time staying detached, that is when It determines you are ready for it.

Joy

The voice, the whisper, the calling, the urge. The desire to know, the desire to remember. The remembrance. The feeling of being lost. The feeling that you've forgotten something. The pulling of your heart to something. The voice in the rain, the whisper in the wind, the stranger in the unknown. The call of my heart. The object of my heart's desire. The essence of my true joy. The face behind the mystery. The mystery unsolved. The depths of the rabbit hole. I want to go deeper into the depths of my insanity, my imagination. I sense that God is there waiting for me. My angel, my shadow. The shadow I always feel lurking around the corners and listening to my conversations. The best friend I've had since I can remember. The friend I would sometimes talk to and have inside jokes with and run crying to when I thought I would die. My invisible friend, who are you? You are not of density are you? You are light and energy aren't you, with the ability to be everywhere at once. That's why I feel you in everything. You are me, you are my mother and my sister, you are my past, and you are my future. I see you, sense you, I feel you every day in my fingertips. I do not know how to explain God, but I believe I have found it in you. Whoever you are, whatever you are, you have given me the greatest gift that anyone could receive. I am grateful to you for this gift. It has given me a new perspective on life. I suddenly feel like I could be everywhere at once. I give you my hand in trust and completeness as I ask you to show me the depths of true compassion and love. My guide, Myself, my God, me. I am. It Is. We are. Us. Joy.

About the Author

Angel (Angelica Irizarry) is an inspirational ambassador, highly intuitive and deeply committed to helping people make lasting, positive changes in their life. She has powerful messenger energy to help people create new emotions, new thoughts, new behaviors, and new realities. She is on a journey to develop the ability to maintain soul consciousness through daily practice of meditation, dance, the performing arts, spiritual relationships and service to humanity.

Angel Irizarry is a new author, creative writer and communicator. Her first published story,

"Nothing Is Beyond Your Reach", is a guide that teaches how to manifest your joy.

http://www.angelicairizarry.com

THE WORM, THE COCOON AND THE BUTTERFLY

Segolene King

It all happened in history class. I was twelve.

Me, and my then love interest, met each other's eyes and magic happened. We were pulled towards each other by a force way beyond our control, wrapped in a swirl of energy that took us up and up to the ceiling, as we came together and kissed. This was my fantasy: a love that was epic, profound and mystical; love that swept you up like a tidal wave.

Did I watch too many movies? Maybe, but at least I was not afraid to dream big.

The great dream did not unfold as planned though. I began the awkward dating game in my mid-teens and on from there, things did not work out. I bumped along a rocky road of fleeting relationships and meaningless flings. I had only one long-term relationship, which became a short-lived, failed attempt at marriage.

I was never the kind of girl to give myself to just anyone, but I did throw myself at some boys who wanted nothing more than what was in between my legs. At best, they were nowhere near ready for the kind of loving devotion and commitment I craved.

So I tried, again and again, to find the right one. I fooled myself into believing that these men were what I needed and ignored the obvious signs of self-deception. I sometimes gave my body, gave my love, gave my power and ended up crashed on the side of the road with a broken heart and badly bruised self-esteem.

For a long time I blamed the men in my life. They just couldn't see I was good for them. They cheated on me and were so obviously lost and confused. Eventually though, when you keep going through similar experiences again and again with various people, you have to wonder: *could it be me?*

What I did not fully realise until later is that I was coming from a space of desperation, need, and wanting to be saved from myself.

As far as I was aware, I just wanted to be loved and happy. Surely, there could be nothing wrong with wanting a big love story, was there?

We human beings are often like icebergs: what we are conscious of is usually only the *tip* of the iceberg. Yet all that other icy stuff under the surface has an effect; has consequences. Back then, I did not see what was under the surface, not yet. I could not help myself. I had this deep need for love and companionship and I had my heart set that I was going to fill it up no matter what.

Little did I know how destructive that could become.

Am I cynical about this? No. In some ways, the desperation and hunger kept me from giving up on love. The desire that drove me was certainly not healthy. It was anchored in a deep hole of loneliness and low self-worth.

I was all messed up inside, so it came out all wrong. Subsequently, I manifested very dubious results.

For those of you who may think life is unfair, let me be honest. If there is one thing I have learnt on my little snapshot of life, it is that the Universe is actually *very fair*. She gives you a perfect reflection of the energy you send out into the world over time. If you don't like the reflection you see in the mirror, don't blame the mirror. Bring it back to yourself. *Own up.* You are the centre and main cause of your life. Once you completely own this, you can start to create change.

In my own learning, Mrs. Universe played her part perfectly, as ever.

I had been seriously committed to my spiritual path for a few years now. With no relationship at all for two of them, I made a priority of the process of personal growth and mastery. This did not mean that the issue was resolved; it was still lurking under the surface, ready to sneak up at the first temptation. But I tried to ignore it.

I saw him for the first time as he barged into the room. I sort of recognised him and remember thinking, "Funny, he's dressed exactly like my ex." The moment passed though, and so did my foreboding.

In the following months I gradually found myself attracted to him. He played the game too. I knew he was no good for me: he was unstable, tortured and drank way too much. He was the type I found all too familiar to my battered heart. Still, I could not help the attraction.

Why?

Because of that unresolved neediness and desperation within me. Though I fought hard against myself, the pit of hunger inside won over.

Eventually, I gave in against all my better judgment. We started a sort of on and off affair that lasted a couple of months. It was nothing serious, but it haunted me. I found myself caught up in an inner battle between attempting to move away from him and wishing it could turn into something more meaningful. I tried and tried to let him go.

On New Year's Eve, we had a huge fight and it was the first of many.

The next day he showed up at my door apologetic. *Could I forgive him? Let him in?* Of course I could. Sucker that I am, I did. And that night we slept together. This was the turning point, though I did not know it yet.

In the following weeks, we fought and fought. I became more emotional, tired, lost appetite and saw my breasts grow bigger and tender. Surely it was because of all the emotional upheaval, wasn't it?

Eventually I had to face reality: *I was pregnant.*

This was one of those 'drop the curtain' moments. I could not believe it. I was both in awe and terrified. I had always wanted children and always envisioned my first pregnancy to be a magical, sacred, joyous occasion. Instead I was confused, alone and faced with a terrible dilemma. I always hoped I would never have to face a decision about terminating a pregnancy. Yet here I was, in an unstable situation emotionally, professionally and financially, with a potential 'father' that was everything I did not want my child's father to be.

I talked to him, but he got angry and refused to even accompany me if I chose to terminate the pregnancy. In fact, he actually had better things to do, like going on a skiing holiday with his ex-girlfriend. Oh, and he was probably going to get back together with her!

And that was it: the straw that broke the camel's back, the last drop, whatever you want to call it. How could I have let my dysfunction go so far? How could I have allowed myself to be used and abused like that?

I did terminate the pregnancy. Although it was a terribly painful and difficult experience, I still feel that it was by far the wisest choice. Most importantly was the sobering process of clearing and growing up that I went through as the result of this experience. I was so over the crap and had gone too far with this nonsense! And so I went through months of intensive personal review, introspection, emotional and psychological clearing work. This time nothing was going to stop me from dropping it once and for all, letting go, changing, and transforming.

I worked my butt off during that time. I took no crap from myself or anyone else, and went into all the dark places I could find inside myself, no matter what they were. Also, as I went through this dark night of the soul, I never lost the faith and vision of a better way. I got my hands dirty, kept my head up, and sorted it out.

Let me make this very clear:

If you want radical change in your life, you have to be ready to change yourself and your behavior, radically. Change only happens with change.

For those of you who like a free lunch and think that a few affirmations or a weekend workshop is going to fix it: get real, go deeper.

It does not have to be as painful as it was for me. It can even be graceful and smooth. No matter what it is, it needs to be deep, committed and real. These things can take time. You cannot become enlightened without shining the light into those dark places. Pretending the dark places are not there is not going to work. You have to be ruthlessly honest with yourself, and fully own up to your life and the mess you may have contributed to. Feel it, let go and commit to do the work of transformation.

When I emerged from that intense period of melting and undoing, I felt at peace. I no longer roamed around with a pit of desperation and need inside. I had accessed my own heart centre and a deeper connection to what I was really about. I felt okay to be me, in my life. I was extremely happy without a relationship at all for however long it would be. I had a sort of certainty that I would be okay and that I could do anything I committed to.

I simply *was*.

This is by no means the end of the journey of course. There is only infinity to go, but it was a huge transformation.

This is when Mrs. Universe poked her nose in with her usual sense of humour and perfect reflection. For the first time in my life, I stopped searching for a relationship, and guess what showed up at my door? Yes, you have it: true love! Mind you, it was not a fall-into-his-arms-and-ride-off-on-his-white-horse scenario. This new man, who is now my wonderful husband and father of my child, was nothing like the others before him. He challenged my beliefs and expectations about love.

This was a good thing.

We had been sort of friends for a while. I had never thought of him in romantic terms. He lived on the other side of the planet, was seventeen years older than me and had three grown up children from a previous marriage. But something was happening. I looked at what I really wanted in my 'perfect man'; he was all that and more.

I dropped the safety net, trusted my deepest heart, and an unimaginable force swirled around us and pulled us together from opposite sides of the world in some sort of magical union. It was mystical, powerful and beautiful all at once.

Sound familiar?

Finally the fantasy from history class came true! I still remember how insane and magical these early days were, and blessed be Mrs. Universe, I thank her every day for bringing us together.

Funnily enough, as I followed my heart and moved to the other side of the planet to be with him, everything else in my life fell into place. I moved into my dream home with a huge garden full of trees. I gained a qualification and started my own business.

Now, I love my work as a life coach and personal growth mentor. I am deeply involved in my process of spiritual and personal growth and have gone through many more transformations. My man and I have never had a fight and any challenge is resolved wisely. Our love seems to have a life of its own, growing beyond what either of us have ever experienced. I have a good life and don't forget the responsibility I have in that. I am so grateful.

Of course life flows on and I now have new dreams. I know I can achieve them. I keep myself honest. I stay true, and I take and learn my lessons. I do my best to live my life in alignment with the guidance of Mrs. Universe. Her and I, we make great partners. And so can you.

About the Author

Segolene is a qualified holistic coach, personal growth mentor, writer and presenter. She is the founder of 'Feminine Source Academy', an online school and coaching/mentoring practice dedicated to women's empowerment, relationship coaching and Sacred Feminine studies. She also is a senior mentor for the 'Insight Foundation', a training and philanthropic organisation dedicated to forging new ways for authenticity, unity and harmony. She has worked with students and clients from various countries since 2004 and offers sessions, online courses, newsletters and workshops.

Originally from France, where she completed a degree in International Business and Languages, Segolene lived and studied in different countries including England, Scotland, Spain and Ireland. She learnt much from the influence of different cultures and explored various career paths, as well as various spiritual paths. It was however not until she came across the 'Insight Foundation' and its 'Integrated Mastery' teachings that she knew she has finally found what she was looking for all along.

Segolene loves to assist others to find and awaken to their true calling and their potential for love, courage and wisdom. She now lives in Western Australia with her family and is currently writing her first novel.

http://www.segolene.com.au

http://www.theinsightfoundation.org.au

LIVING THE SCIENCE OF GETTING RICH

Croz Crossley

It is strange thinking back to the time when I thought my world had fallen apart, but I can assure you that the feelings I had then were very real. Changing my circumstances seemed like an impossible task.

What happened?

Well I had a very large company that supplied security staff and in an effort to take things a bit easier, I trained a star employee to run day-to-day activities. I eventually made him a Director of the company. During this time he became a close family friend. The reason for making him a Director was two-fold. Number one, it was a reward for his input, and two, I thought that by making him my business partner and part owner of the company, I would secure his position within the organisation.

Things went well for a time, and as my new partner did more, I gave him access to more and more behind the scenes information. It appeared to be a match made in heaven. I was giving him the benefit of my advice, and he was doing a great job implementing the information, while at the same time learning some real business skills. Life was good. We had a wonderful Christmas that year and he and his wife were our guests, and accepted as part of our family.

Then suddenly on January 6th, I got a letter from one of our major contracts informing me that they were cancelling our contract and going to use the services of another company. I then received a phone call from another company we did work for and got the same message. I tried to ring my partner to see what he knew. At this time I did not associate him at all with what was happening. It would have been inconceivable that he could be involved: I had given him everything, and he was like a son to me.

During the course of the morning eighty percent of our clients rang and said that they were going with this new company. By lunchtime the whole sorry state of affairs had unraveled. My partner had gone to every client telling them that he was starting a company and could supply the doormen for a cheaper rate. As he knew everything about our behind the scenes structure, he could offer exactly the same service. He even had intimate knowledge of our systems, and the key part was that he was their direct contact. He was going to be the new company.

I can hear you all screaming 'get the lawyers!' and I assure you I did contact one, who gave me some of the best advice I had ever got from a lawyer. That was, 'wipe your face and get on with your life'. I assure you that was not what I wanted to hear. Although I had a good case using a thing called 'fiduciary duties' (a Director's duty to a company), the lawyer said that the case would prove very costly and could also be very protracted. He actually said that a lawyer fresh out of university would be able to muck about with a case like this for up to seven years, so you can imagine what a tricky lawyer could do.

To cut a long story short, after working hard for many years and at forty plus years of age, my wife and I were looking at a very bleak future. To say we were devastated would be an understatement; *we were gutted*. Over the next few weeks, the extent of what had happened became even more evident. As a knock on effect of cutting off our cash flow, we lost everything. As all the debt had to be repaid, all our savings had to be used to satisfy creditors and banks and eventually the ultimate nail in the coffin: we had to sell our house to settle even more debt.

It would seem that we were not very well structured. It amazed me how quickly people start grabbing your assets when things go wrong. With no income, we could not deal with creditors by offering a payment plan. We were gone, and it was very difficult to work out what we were going to do.

The next month or two was a nightmare and the more we looked into the future, the worse it looked. We were not sleeping and every decision we made seemed to be wrong. Our minds were scrambled. During this time, when we were moving, I noticed a book that had been given to me a few years before called 'The Science of Getting Rich'. I had read it briefly at that time, but not taken very much notice of it. One sentence I remembered from it entered my head, "If you follow the instructions in this book, you cannot fail to get rich." I smiled and thought, "Have I got a test for you?"

Looking back, at this point I learnt one of the most important things about manifesting, and that is…

You must make the commitment with yourself to do what is necessary and to stay focused until that thing appears.

Obviously that is not all you need to do, but it is essential that you make that commitment.

My wife and I said that we had nothing to lose, so we decided to read the book and do exactly as we were instructed. I think this was the first time in my life I was going to do *exactly* as I was told. It is funny how focused you can become when you are desperate. It is obviously much better to make decisions to change your life when things are not desperate: they still work just the same, and you don't have to experience the grief.

We read the book through a couple times out loud, and while certain things resonated, I must say that other things didn't. We had made a pledge however, and in all fairness if we did not do things *exactly*, then we would have no right to comment at the end if things did not turn out as we had hoped.

The next few weeks were really strange. I think the main thing this had given us was hope. That in itself had changed our mindset from one of looking into the future seeing despair, to one of seeing good things and numerous possibilities.

When you are really low, it is so important to get something to focus on, that is the first thing. You must then have faith and belief in achieving what you are focusing on. That focus gives you a route and destination out of your predicament.

One of the things you are told to do in 'The Science of Getting Rich' is to create a clear mental image of what you want to achieve. It also said that you should feel now what it would be like when you get there. This was one thing that really tested us, because it was very difficult to actually feel happy and wealthy when the reality was that we were desperate and broke. I must admit though that when I could do it, that is *feel* the situation I was envisaging, things felt good. It seemed that things in the real world tuned into this feeling. We turned this into a bit of an exercise and noticed that without any doubt, when we felt happy and content, everything seemed to go well, and when we slipped back into our misery, that was exactly how the outside world responded.

We were making a little progress, and as we got more control over this simple exercise, the quicker it seemed we could change our circumstances. We found that this effect was a roll over effect. As we got more control over it, the longer the periods of well-being continued. Once we had firmly established that it was actually our mindset that was starting the process, and we were able to feel and see what happened when we felt right, we could then start looking at the other parts of the puzzle.

The book listed many things that had to be done to ensure we stayed on track. It was called living in the 'Certain Way'.

THE KEY ELEMENTS TO LIVING IN A CERTAIN WAY

1. Know what you want specifically and definitely.

2. See yourself already in possession of it, and enjoy it now.

3. Contemplate daily on the clear mental picture.

4. Realize in grateful faith that it is yours.

5. Act from the creative mind, not the competitive mind.

6. Act *now* in an efficient way.

7. Remember it is both thoughts and actions that create results.

Suffice to say, things went from good to better and then on to amazing. When we wrote out our vision, everything on it seemed like a real stretch. It included a property portfolio exceeding three million dollars, a new company in a totally different industry, world travel on extended time frames and many other things that have all been achieved and surpassed in the years that followed. There was one thing in the vision we put as a little treat, and that was to travel around the USA in a huge recreational vehicle for six months, stopping in different places and meeting interesting people. That adventure is locked in for next year, and I will also be stopping and talking to groups of people teaching them what I found out about these teachings.

There are so many people out there selling snake oil and the next get rich quick scheme, so let me just give you my observations. Firstly, there is no such thing as a get rich quick scheme, although many people earn lots of money selling that dream. Secondly, if you read everything about how to change your life you will get confused, so find one teaching that you trust and just stick with that until you succeed. Thirdly, once you set your goal and have faith and belief in it arriving, nothing can stop you. Lastly, just dreaming will do nothing but frustrate you. If you want to create and realize your vision, you must use inspired *action*.

When I first read this book, it was a bit difficult because it was written in a style from over one hundred years ago and also included words that we no longer use. So a few years ago I rewrote the book and called it 'The Science of Getting Rich in Plain English,' which I have made available on my website. The book also contains tips and advice on how to make the teachings work for you.

In conclusion, I can only say that it is possible to change your life, simply by changing the way you look at it. Do not expect immediate success, but rest assured that if you do things correctly, you can manifest anything you desire. I hope this short story will give you the inspiration and motivation to follow your dreams. As a post script I would mention that as a result of my commitment to these teachings, I have found it in me to totally forgive my former business partner: and that my friends, is another wonderful story, perhaps for another time.

About the Author

Guardian of **Worry Free Island**. Author, speaker, writer and guide to entrepreneurs, individuals and business, with a spiritual twist.

http://www.croz.com.au

FROM FAT TO SLIM WITH EASE AND GRACE

Glenn Groves

Fat. I was fat. I had been fat for years. I had gone from being over-weight to being fat to being obese for nearly twenty years, from my early twenties to forty. I seemed to have almost no control over my weight. I knew what to do to lose it – eat less and move more. I tried doing that in different ways. I tried different diets – low calorie, low carbohydrate, meal replacement sachets, pre-packaged and home delivered. I even tried just eating smallish amounts of healthy food.

They all worked – *as long as I followed them.* The problem was that I seemed to be incapable of following any method for long. As soon as I stopped, I would go back to my old ways of eating, and the weight would come back.

What would happen is that any time I started either dieting or eat-ing healthily, I would start to get bad feelings like sadness, worry, or being trapped. These feelings would slowly grow stronger and stron-ger and would only go away once I started eating bad food again. I would resist the feeling for a while – sometimes minutes, sometimes days, sometimes even weeks. As long as I resisted it, I would follow the diet or eat well, and my weight would decrease. But eventually I would give in to the feeling and eat bad food again – and lots of it! This is what kept me fat.

I had no chance of losing weight or of staying slim once I *had* lost the weight while the negative emotions kept arising. It was almost like something inside me was pushing me to be fat and stay that way... something pushing me away from being slim. I *knew* what to do to lose weight. In fact, losing it was easy when I did what I knew to do. This was not a question of knowledge though. I suspect that every-one who is fat knows what to do... they just don't do it.

I was no different.

I used to feel embarrassed or ashamed of how I looked, thinking, "Other people can control their weight, what is wrong with me that I cannot control mine? Am I weak?" I felt like I was not really living life, like this was just a practice run, and maybe one day I would start really living. While my weight was only part of that, it was the most obvious.

How could I control or be in charge of any part of my life when I had no control over something so simple?

The Power of Visualisation

Fortunately, a friend of mine shared with me the concept of visualisation: seeing what you want to have and how you want to be. She showed that when you visualise and feel good about what you are seeing, you naturally move towards it.

I started to visualise slim.

When I first started, I couldn't see *myself* as slim. I tried to use my imagination to see a picture of myself that way, but instead saw a picture of myself as fat. So I was stuck. How could I visualise slim when my mind seemed so determined to see me as fat? Fortunately, there was a simple answer – *whatever we see and feel good about is what we move towards.*

It does not even have to be ourselves that we are seeing. So I chose someone that I knew was slim (and healthy and happy) and visualised him. Because he always had a big, genuine smile, I also felt good while seeing him.

Finally I was seeing slim!

Whenever I had spare time, I would see and visualise this 'slim and happy' guy! Over the next few days, the bad feeling – the one that drove me to eat bad food – started to decrease … *and soon disappeared.*

Sticking to a diet of healthy food and eating fewer calories than I used up each day became easy. I no longer had to fight the emotion that was pushing me to eat bad food. After years of fighting the battle of weight, I won it, and finally achieved a healthy weight I hadn't been since I was a teenager.

Now, I like how I look and I like how I feel. I feel proud when I walk down the street and meet people. I feel confident in a way I never did before. I feel like I have a say in how my life goes... like I am no longer at the whim of whatever circumstances happen to me or whatever emotions I feel. This is partly because of my weight loss, and partly because I practice visualisation.

Once I produced good results for myself using visualisation, I started to wonder what goes on inside our heads when we visualise. And through investigation I learned the specific answers as to why it is such a powerful technique...

The Conscious and Subconscious Mind

We have two parts to our minds – the conscious, and the subconscious. We are mainly aware of our conscious mind, hence the name (we are *conscious* of it), and mainly unaware of our subconscious mind, hence the prefix *'sub'*. Since it is below our conscious awareness, it is our *sub* (or below) *conscious* mind.

Our subconscious exists to keep us alive. It does things like keep our heart beating, lungs breathing, and our kidneys filtering (or whatever it is that kidneys do!). But that is not all our subconscious does. It also tries to keep us safe from danger, and often succeeds. The way it keeps us safe seems a bit weird at first, but once you do fully understand, it does make sense.

Imagine you are inside a building and you want to leave it. There are three corridors to choose from. You *cannot see* down the first corridor at all – You *can see* down the second corridor, but it *feels bad* – And you *can see* down the third corridor, and it *feels good*. Which corridor do you choose?

Almost everyone would choose the corridor that they can see down and feels good. That's because our subconscious keeps us safe from danger by only letting us go where we can see (where we can also notice and avoid dangers). If we go where we cannot see, then we are blind to dangers and cannot avoid them (and are more likely to be harmed). If we can see different things, then we go towards whichever feels best. This is why our subconscious mind exists: to keep us safe and alive by directing us only to where we can see.

To summarize, our subconscious mind uses these two 'rules of thumb' to keep us safe:

1. We only go where we can see.

2. If we can see different ways to go, then we go the way that feels best.

When I say that our subconscious only lets us 'go' somewhere, I mean both physical places and circumstances. Being fat or slim, happy, having plenty of money and having great friends are all circumstances...

The Language of Emotion

Our subconscious talks to us using emotion (the only language it speaks) to keep us safe:

- When it wants us to change what we are doing or what we are heading towards, it makes us feel bad. Since we do not like feeling bad, we change what we are doing or where we are heading.

- When our subconscious wants us to keep doing what we are doing or keep heading in the same direction, it makes us feel good. Since we like feeling good, we keep doing what we are doing or keep heading in that direction.

We can use visualisation combined with how we feel to talk to our subconscious.

Most of how we feel, behave and act comes from our subconscious. By visualizing and feeling good about what you want to be, do, and have, you let your subconscious see those things. When your subconscious sees those things, and you feel good about them, it thinks they are safe. And because it wants to keep you safe, it will then take you in the direction of those things. By using visualisation, you attract yourself towards what you want so that it becomes natural for you to move towards it. This is partly why this is called the Law of Attraction.

Everything you've read here is the fundamental psychology behind visualisation. There is more to visualisation and the Law of Attraction than just this aspect of psychology, however even if it were all you ever understood, you can probably see how visualisation is an incredibly powerful tool for creating our lives as we would love them to be. Ultimately, visualisation allows us to create who we are and where we are heading from the inside out, so that naturally, we move towards what is important to us, and do so with ease and grace.

About the Author

My name is Glenn Groves, I was raised in New Zealand, and currently reside in the beautiful city of Sydney, Australia. My university studies included psychology, and I have continued to study practical psychology on a part-time basis since that time.

By "practical psychology" I mean stuff to do with how human beings and our minds work, what it takes to be happy now, to love life now, to enjoy life now, and to be moving towards circumstances that we would love to have. Practical psychology works with tools that people can use to enhance their everyday lives, as opposed to "curative psychology" which deals with breakdowns or things that go wrong inside our minds.

I have combined psychology with computer software, to create software that can, to an extent, think for itself. This combination has been granted a patent, and has won an award for innovation.

I have trained to lead seminars, and have been involved in running seminars and coaching in the personal development area since 1997. I have spoken at conferences and meetings both in Australia and the United States, and I am a member of Mensa Australia.

In my spare time I cuddle my cute dog (a Jack Russell cross, from the RSPCA), walk, sometimes run, read a lot, spend time with friends, enjoy driving my slightly rare American car (rare in Australia anyway), and regularly threaten 10 innocent pins with a heavy ball in a bowling alley. I also make jokes that are occasionally recognised as such.

http://www.thefutureisfreedom.com

THE GLOBAL BUTTERFLY

Katie Joy

The first hairline crack in the egg of evolution I came out of began in 1996. My family of two parents and two younger brothers lived as most Australians do; paycheck-to-paycheck. In our case, as dad was rather entrepreneurial, it had been a roller coaster ride of some money coming in, then periods of drought.

Since he was always working hard, I hardly spent much time with him – and when he was around, he was grumpy, stressed, and seemingly angry with life.

While I now have a great relationship with my father, this one particular day when I was sixteen I had a standing row with him where I was vying for his attention. As usual, he was busy handling life, business, and his own emotions. The poor man could hardly breathe and in the heat of the moment, through his own frustration, he backhanded me.

Shocked and angry, I cried, "I will never be broke or poor! I will be wildly wealthy!"

That moment has stuck with me ever since.

At the time, what I wanted most from my father was his attention, approval and love. You know, those simple things that make us feel valuable. Little did I know how much that one experience would permeate my conscious and subconscious, as my story will soon reveal…

In 1999, I met a special man, who within a short week of coming to visit me in Perth had proposed and stayed. He never went back to his home town of Sydney, and we got married April of 2000. He adored me. He loved me. And he was also in debt. So I worked on managing that, along with my own finances and borrowings.

The marriage however was destined to fail.

It was built on 'being accepted and loved' but I didn't have an eternal heart for him. While we soon moved forward from debt and into our first house – In 2002, we separated and later divorced.

By this time I had been working for St John Ambulance for a few years, beginning as a Transport Officer in 2000. In 2002 I began my career as an Ambulance Officer and later graduated as a Paramedic.

During my first roster on the road, I was partnered with a senior Paramedic as a tutor. He was authoritarian, tall, protective, self-assured and pursued me. Our relationship flourished and in 2005 we got married. Like my previous husband, he too was in debt, this time though with a much larger amount. I felt for us to move forward, we needed to clear the debt and then use our money to invest, and so I helped him fix that too.

In 2005 I moved to Port Hedland with my husband, who was promoted to a Station Manager role. At the time of going I had no role to step into. Considering I had just qualified as a Senior Paramedic the year before, it was a big leap of faith for me.

He made a promise though that we would only go for his two-year term, and then we'd move back to Perth after that.

That promise was fractured the day we moved: I was unpacking a box, pulling out an elephant carving stand with its back shaped flat as a small table. As I sat on the lounge, my 6'7" husband stood over me rubbing his hands together and said, "Now imagine what it'll be like living here for five or seven years!"

I briefly ran a visual of whacking him in the head with the carving! I was so mad! I felt tricked, deceived, isolated and a long way from home; 1,800 kilometers to be exact. He got what he wanted without caring what I wanted, so it seemed.

With the relationship dissolving since the trust was blown, I began swaying between hope and insistence over the next few years of holding my husband accountable to his promise, and moving towards creating financial freedom. I wanted this so I could not only move away from Port Hedland with my marriage intact, but also set myself up so I never had to work again if I didn't want to.

With all this trouble stirred up in my mind, it was no wonder I had countless sleepless nights. I would wake up in the early hours of the morning with my subconscious putting the pieces of the jigsaw together. I'd take what was said to me as truth. All the while my subconscious was working on the information while I slept, and like a diligent secretary would hand me a file upon awakening. A picture of truth would be laid out. I didn't want to admit that my marriage was going to fail. Not another one! That challenged my ego. I didn't want to 'fail' again!

In early 2006 I was up at 3 am with one of my episodes of insomnia. Of all things, my habit would be to iron in front of the TV. I was tuned into one of the late-night shopping channels and up boomed Anthony Robbins with his 'Get the Edge' CD collection. Enthralled, glued to the TV and with my hand on the phone waiting for the number to dial, I prayed this would work. As a last hope, I ordered it and went to bed, with the ironing unfinished, and a heart full of hope.

Within a few weeks the package arrived. I had mentioned to my husband what I had bought and set a proviso that we both must share in the learning together, or I was leaving. We'd also recently watched "The Secret," which really set my intentions in motion and on fire!

My primary goal was to create enough passive income to replace my working income. With my new goals and clarity of path, I had set my intention to purchase two positive cash-flow properties within two weeks! That was created. I also set my intention and self into action to write and publish a cookbook. I completed that within nine weeks!

Unfortunately, my marriage was dissolving, rapidly.

The second beginning of my awakening began in 2007, a few months before my thirty-second birthday. The crumbling of my second marriage manifested in separation, and later that year I moved back to

Perth, Western Australia. I set my sights on a new goal: to become a global citizen with multiple streams of passive income, and no anchor in any one location.

During my time with my husband, I had helped shape our finances from minus $250,000 (debt) to over $1.3 million in just over five years. After we separated, we halved everything, making my personal net worth now $655,000. With my financial thermostat now set at $1.3 million, I decided to move forward with my wealth creation. Within only six months I recreated my property portfolio, set my net wealth back up to $1.3 million and achieved my goal to replace my working income with passive income.

In March 2008, I retired as a Paramedic and decided to invest in me by becoming a full-time traveler and Adventurepreneur!

During the previous months, I had done some soul-searching. Why had I attracted two men into my life that were in debt? What hadn't worked? What did I need to change? I realised that I was the common denominator, and that the change needed to come from within me.

It was during a healing process in December of that same year that I became aware of a subconscious belief that had been driving my life. Having revisited my memory of that emotional day with my father when I was sixteen years old, I realized that when I had been smacked, I not only made the promise to be wildly wealthy, I had also subconsciously linked 'no money = no love'. From that day forward, my life spun and took on a new direction.

Since March of 2008, I have traveled the world on many adventures: USA, Peru, The Amazon, Argentina, Antarctica, Uruguay, Hawaii, Fiji, India, Bali, UK, Europe, the Caribbean, and all over Australia. During these journeys I have met many people who have helped me to reshape and change my life. I've been mentored and coached by many of the masters in their fields: Mark Victor Hansen, Bill Bartmann, Anthony Robbins, Jeff Walker, and Steve Linder, to name just a few.

I would follow my heart and listen to the internal voice gently nudging me (sometimes loud and clear) for which steps to take next. The hardest leap of faith was my initial one – letting go of the illusionary security of my job and to do what my heart and soul most called me to do: travel the world.

The day I put my resignation in I was greeted with great relief and awareness that I was about to embark on an incredible journey – And I have, with far more greatness than I could have even imagined when I first began! From getting out there and working on me, meeting people and expanding my comfort zone, so many doors have opened up.

Many people have asked me along the way, "How have you created your amazing life?" When I've shared my financial strategy, I've witnessed some people smile with awe, while many others pulled back with a resignation of "I can't do that." So for a while, I stopped telling people what I did, and just lived my life as a light and the embodiment of what one can create, be, do and have in their life.

On New Year's Eve 2010, while spending the evening with my dear friend Cat, and working on our tradition of renewing our vision board and goals, I made a decision. I felt the calling so strongly inside that 2011 was going to become the year I make a difference globally in people's lives. I wanted to find a way to demonstrate the principles of creating a lifestyle by design. I just didn't know yet how I was going to do that exactly.

Four days later while at Brisbane International airport, getting ready to board my flight to Los Angeles, I came across a magazine in the news agency. I flicked through it and turned to a double page article titled 'One Red Paperclip'. It told the true story of a Canadian called Kyle McDonald who, in 2005, began a trading game with one red paperclip. He traded up for bigger or better items until he got to his goal of his final trade for a house. He did that inside one year exactly, with a total of fourteen trades!

My body vibrated with goose bumps. This was my intuition letting me know this was my inspiration for how I was going to share my story and empower others to create the life of their dreams too! I decided to create the 'Global Trading Game', beginning with a packet of Tim Tams (chocolate cookies) and set my goal to trade up for items that were bigger or better as I traveled around the world. I decided for my end goal: to trade up for a position on Sir Richard Branson's Virgin Galactic, to experience going to outer space!

I began my trade publicly with a blog, rapidly tapping it out on my computer as I sat at the departure gate. I hit send on my blog article and boarded my plane knowing that my life had changed forever, and that I was about to impact a lot of people's lives world-wide.

At the time of writing this story, I'm currently at Trade Six – a $47,000 'Wealth Creation' package, and have traded in five countries around the world.

In January, while on an internet marketer's cruise in the Caribbean, I met a man who sat next to me on the bus of a 'Highlights of Curucao' while touring the island. He was from the internet marketer's group too. We got chatting and when I shared with him my goals for the Global Trading Game and raising a million dollars for Virgin Unite, he grinned and said, "I'm going to Necker Island next month to spend a week with Richard Branson. Perhaps I'll put in a good word for you." Almost a week later, with the expansion of our friendship, he invited me to join him to meet Sir Richard Branson. I accepted!

So in February, I spent a week with my biggest mentor, all because I visualised my goals and desires! I'm still on my path of fulfilling my final vision: to be on Virgin Galactic and to globally raise the million dollars.

It's the journey that counts, the people you meet and the experiences you have. Pay attention to all the messages the Universe gives you as you go along your path. Everything you want is within you right now.

First imagine it, believe and then take action!

About the Author

Katie Joy is a globetrotter, traveling the world sprinkling her magic wherever she goes; breathing life and enthusiasm into those she meets with her enlightened perspectives, personal experiences, and sense of candid humour; educating with practical steps to create the life of your dreams. She energizes people into action with her effervescent joy. Her vivacious yet grounded presence brings forth teachings with fun, laughter, joy and new insights to see the gifts each person has in life. Her exceptional view of life, philosophy and enlightened understanding of how to create life on your own terms is transforming the lives of millions. As a researcher, writer, speaker, life coach, philosopher and retired paramedic, her studies and life experiences have made her a leading expert on how to consciously create your ideal lifestyle by design; healing, human potential and philosophy.

Katie Joy retired in 2008 at age thirty-two. She's been traveling the world full-time since, visiting some of the most exotic and sometimes adventurous spots in the world, and hanging out with some of the biggest movers and shakers. A self-made millionaire, twice over, Katie Joy lives the life of her dreams with those she loves. It is a remarkable life!

http://www.TheGlobalButterfly.com

DO WHAT YOU LOVE

Kylah Morrison

Keen to See the World

As I step down onto the tarmac and remove my helmet, the adrenalin rushes through my body. Flying an F18 fighter jet is exhilarating and I get a rush every time we go to the Southern Alps of New Zealand on training missions.

But, I'm not a fighter pilot.

My dream to become one was sadly extinguished when the New Zealand government decommissioned all the jets in the Air Force to become a Defence Force. I had just finished school and quickly had to find another career path to pursue. Fortunately, dreams or visions can be fairly fluid. They often change based on the experiences we have and the people we meet. Unsure about what it was I wanted to do in life, I decided to enroll in university in the hope that the answer would present itself there.

Like most school graduates from small country towns I couldn't wait to live in the big smoke and so I moved down south to commence my university studies in Christchurch. Being more of an all-rounder (rather than excelling in one particular area), I fell into engineering purely because I was good at math and science, but also because a friend's older brother was studying it.

Little did I know that within only nine years of leaving school I would find myself traveling to Paris to represent New Zealand at the 'International Institute of Women in Engineering' and go on to work on offshore drilling rigs and gas platforms around New Zealand and

Australia. I would meet an amazing, supportive guy and move back to a small town, this time in outback Australia. There the dirt is red and blue skies stretch as far as the eye can see!

It's funny how life turns out sometimes.

As the years progressed at university, my ideas for the future changed from wanting to be a fighter pilot in the Air Force, to designing heart valves and knee joints in the bio-medical industry, to finally a position in senior management of an international oil and gas company. That was it: I'd discovered my new dream. Or so I thought. As long as I can remember though, I've believed that people can only be truly successful in life if they are passionate about what they do.

When I was fifteen years old we had to interview someone we found inspiring for a school project. I chose New Zealand's first female fighter pilot Kellie Logue. I was thrilled when she invited me to interview her on site at Ohakea Airbase. I can still remember the day I stood on the top step of her fighter jet. I wasn't able to climb in because that privilege was reserved only for the Prime Minister and trained fighter pilots, but I could feel excitement and adrenalin as I imagined what it might be like to step over the threshold and into the cockpit. Later, the sensation of flying in the training simulator through the Manawhatu Gorge was a thousand times better than any rides I'd been on at the local fair. I decided then and there that if I could become a fighter pilot, I'd be in heaven!

When that was no longer an option, I eventually translated my dream of being a fighter pilot into being in senior management of an international oil and gas company without really thinking about why I wanted to pursue such a dream. There are elements of my job which I love, but those earlier beliefs I had about successful people being passionate about what they do, have come back to challenge me. The fighter pilot of my youth has gone but there is a new dream on the horizon!

After much soul searching and thinking about what makes me happiest in my work life, I have recently identified that I am passionate about business excellence. My dream is to have a career that supports and inspires people to excel in business, whatever their chosen venture may be. Some of the most valuable advice I've received so far that has helped me take those crucial steps towards achieving my goals has been to:

1. Know and follow my heart,

2. Take control of my destiny, and

3. Talk to people who inspire me

In the following sections I'll outline the journey I took to refine my dream into something I'm truly passionate about, with the hope of providing inspiration to others!

Look Inward and Believe

Struggling with conflicting ambitions to fly jets, explore the world, and have a successful career, I embarked on my first personal development course in 2006. For me the most valuable lessons from this were the importance of self-awareness, identifying my core values, describing my vision and setting SMART (Specific, Measureable, Achievable, Realistic and Time-based) goals in order to work towards my vision. Personal development is an iterative process and I've often reflected on these lessons, each time further refining my authentic dream.

Self Awareness

This course was the first time I had ever written a journal. My sister had a journal when we were growing up, but I didn't see the point of writing down the entire goings on of the day, including who liked who and what I was thinking. Letters written in class and neatly folded into tiny envelopes satisfied those teenage interests for me. It was only when I had to keep a journal for this course and later came across the technique of free writing that I realised the value of journaling.

Free writing, a form of journaling where you don't focus on getting coherent sentences on paper, allows you to brain dump quickly and effectively. I find this technique far easier than traditional journaling. It gets all my concerns out of my head and onto paper, which seems to lighten the load. On paper things don't appear so daunting. Journaling is also a great way to look back at the progress I've made towards my goals.

Identifying Core Values

Identifying my core values was hard, but revisiting them over time to see whether they are truly what I stand for and desire has helped me to define them better. I assess whether they are guiding me on my journey towards being passionate about what I do. Knowing what drives me and then being able to align that with the work I do day-to-day has alleviated a lot of stress for me. It has also helped me identify why certain things upset or frustrate me.

Having defined my values, living them was the next challenge. It is rare that our work and other aspects of life will satisfy all our core values at once. I know that there will be times when some of my values will be more prominent in different situations or stages of life but I still struggle with this. For example, I value a challenge and continual learning. I also value balance. At times I'm so motivated and driven to understand something new that I will neglect good habits like regular exercise, reading, or drinking enough water, in pursuit of the short term goal. I have to stop and remind myself to find my happy medium again.

Identifying Strengths

Using a self-assessment test and feedback from colleagues at work I have identified my top five strengths: Creativity, Curiosity, Leadership, Fairness, and Love of Learning. This exercise helped me understand why some things that take me days to complete might only take hours for someone else.

One of the biggest lessons I've learned since commencing work is that everyone has strengths in different areas and no one can expect to be good at everything. I often beat myself up about not being a 'good' engineer because I don't do the calculations as quickly as others. Now I realize that my strengths lie in other areas. I'm a 'big picture' thinker and I am creative. I can see how things impact each other and I can effectively communicate that to the different people involved. A more analytical, typically calculation oriented engineer may not. Armed with this knowledge, I make sure that I mix up more technical tasks with creative tasks so that I'm giving my brain a break and re-energizing it.

Look after Yourself

Know and nurture the strengths you have. They will help you follow your dreams.

Take Control

'Don't ask. Don't get'. This was what one of the guys working in the workshop at my summer job said to me one day and I'll never forget it. Stuck in the office, printing labels for an inventory of all the workshop tools, I was itching to get out on site and see what the 'coal face' was like. One afternoon, after at least two attempts at picking up the phone, I finally rang my boss and asked him if I could go on site with the field service technicians so that I could get a better understanding of the business. His reply, "Sure, why don't you see if they can take you with them this afternoon?" I was stunned and surprised. I couldn't believe my luck! Winging it, taking a risk and asking for something I really wanted, despite assuming I'd get a negative response, had paid off. From that day forward I've made a promise to myself to ask the question, difficult or otherwise.

Ask the Questions

Take the risk. What's the worst that can happen? Someone may say no but you're still better off asking because it stops you wasting time wondering and you may get a nice surprise. I've learnt that putting off the difficult questions or phone calls usually makes it harder, so now I try to act as soon as possible.

Control Your Destiny

You are the only person who has ultimate control of your own destiny. If you are not happy, do something about it, but give any change a chance to manifest its positive elements. A good piece of advice I got was to wait three months. If you are not happy with your current position, identify the issues and work at making a difference through small changes day-to-day. If at the end of the three months you are still not happy, re-assess your options and take action.

Network and Prosper

Most of my decisions about changes in my career direction to date have been as a result of talking to people. People are usually flattered when you approach them for advice. With great success, I've used email, phone and face-to-face approaches to make contact with people such as inspiring presenters, writers or just people that someone else has recommended that I talk to. As my network grows, each approach is easier than the last.

I was surprised how many people didn't, and still don't know what it is they really want to do. This brings a smile to my face and makes me think of the Sunscreen song;

> *"Don't feel guilty if you don't know what you want to do with your life… the most interesting people I know didn't know at twenty-two what they wanted to do with their lives, some of the most interesting 40 year olds I know still don't."*

Like happiness, I've decided my career is more of a journey than a destination, providing challenges and frustration as well as satisfaction and fulfillment. While continually learning new lessons, it is shaping me into a more whole person.

Build a Network

A couple of books I've read recently, Sarah Prout's *'The Power of Influence'* and *"The 4-hr Work Week"* by Tim Ferriss, have motivated me to go out of my comfort zone to contact some key people who inspire me. I'm finally taking the steps to manifest what I've yearned for since leaving university.

I've created my own website – rather daunting at first but taking baby steps has helped – and I've started blogging about the things I'm passionate about. After less than two months I'm already seeing results both in this domain and in my day job. It is a very pleasant surprise to see how quickly these results have come into fruition!

A supportive network is key to delivering the encouragement and kick up the backside you need to get after your dreams.

World's Your Oyster

If I could offer advice to anyone who is starting out on their career or considering a change, it would be to identify your core values and your strengths, then spend time refining your vision. Make sure it is something that motivates you to get out of bed every morning. What activities do you do where time seems to fly and you don't notice it passing? What events, smells, tastes evoke the happiest memories for you? How do you imagine your perfect workday to be?

Focus on those things and how you can make them occur more frequently in your life. Understand too that you may not walk into the job of your dreams; it takes a lot of hard work, an element of confidence and periodic self-reflection along the journey. Be true to yourself, embrace the journey and have fun!

About the Author

Kylah Morrison, a qualified Engineer, commenced her career in the oil and gas industry without really understanding what motivated her, or what she was passionate about. After Kylah's dream to become a fighter pilot was taken away from her, it took much self-reflection and continual growth to refine a new dream.

Inspired by companies that have been truly successful because of their organisational culture and the way they operate, Kylah is embarking on a journey to realise her passion for business excellence, living her core values and making the most of her strengths.

http://www.kylahmorrison.com

CREATING A LIFE OF ABUNDANCE

Evelyn Lim

While running on the treadmill of life, we can often find ourselves in trouble if we don't stop to question. We fail to gain the awareness that an overemphasis on materialism could hardly be called true wealth.

A Dream to Make Lots of Cash

I have the dream to live a life of abundance. However, I used to believe that being abundant simply meant having lots of money.

We find ourselves in trouble should we never stop to question while running on the treadmill of life. We would not have gained the awareness that an overemphasis on materialism could hardly be called true wealth. I have the dream to live a life of abundance. However, I used to believe that being abundant simply meant having lots of money.

I come from Singapore, a cosmopolitan island-city in South-East Asia and the world's fourth leading financial center. Life had been pretty much a rat race, with a focus on accomplishments. The banking environment that I was in for close to ten years was highly competitive. Everyone around, including my parents, friends and colleagues worked their butt off in order to afford the ever-increasing cost of living.

The aspiration to succeed has often been fueled by our government's frequent calls for its country to be world-class. While I was growing up in the '80s, our local papers made the observation of a typical Singaporean's excessive obsession with materialistic desires. It was summed up as the dream of the 5Cs: Cash, Condo, Car, Credit Card and Country Club Membership.

Till today, many place their hopes on attaining the 5 Cs. It is an important benchmark to meet as it indicates success – that is, we have *made it* in life. There is a constant pursuit to be successful, be at the top or be the very best, lest we be left behind. So life is pretty much a hub of tasks centered on making money, ensuring that we stay high on productivity levels and competing for top rankings.

The result is that we don't realize how empty we feel inside because we are too busy filling our days with breakneck activities. Rather, we get so used to the underlying numbness that we don't recognize the fact that something is amiss. This was what happened to me for a long time.

Being in the banking industry at the start of my career opened my eyes to what money could possibly buy. I was also very fortunate in having a fast-track job that would bring material comforts. However, depending on my salary alone was not enough for me. Motivated by greed, I punted on stocks repeatedly and during the financial crisis, lost a lot of my savings.

The trigger finally came in the form of maternal instincts. I got married and had children. Suddenly, I realized that I wanted to be the main caregiver to my girls as soon as they were born. And so I made the choice that differed from the norm of a dual-income family. The decision to quit my job surprised many of my friends. Even my parents questioned the soundness of my decision.

Turning Points to an Authentic Dream of Abundance

Still, getting to know what my true dream of abundance looked like did not happen overnight. Having financial wealth was important, but I began to desire balance. For a start, I recognized that time was a precious commodity. The thought of being able to work flexible hours through starting a part-time business became appealing as the arrangement would allow greater bonding time with my children.

The move to entrepreneurship was not easy. I had a couple of false starts. I spent thousands of dollars attending workshops. At first, I was drawn to the blinking lights of touted promises in making money quick and fast. I even participated in an online scam, on the mistaken belief that it was my ticket to financial freedom.

I must have sent out conflicting signals to the Universe. Even after I set my first intention in becoming an entrepreneur, I was like a swinging yo-yo, changing my mind from one day to the next. My journey to financial freedom began to reveal the negative consequences of my core issues. I was miserable, frustrated, and stressed out.

The grass always looked greener than from where I was standing. It did not matter that we could live comfortably even on the single income of my husband. I was just too focused on the lack – my insecurities. My self-esteem crashed when I gave up having an independent paycheck. To earn it back, I wanted to make money fast. And so I moved from one venture to the next... with little success.

As I had not been getting the results I wanted, I realized that it was time to do something different. I was getting sick and tired of listening to the same stories that I had been telling myself. Filled with self-pity, criticism and blame, they had the single theme of negativity.

Fortunately, I came upon the movie *The Secret*. It highlighted the need to master the mind before mastering one's life. It offered hope to the discontent that I was experiencing. Something inside me clicked. Enough was enough, I finally decided! Even while I had previously understood the importance of positive thinking, I was moved into real action only after watching the movie.

And so, I set the intent to live a life of abundance, one that would be balanced in mind-body-spirit. Since the search outside had not led me to fulfillment, I decided to start from the beginning – the source of my problems. In a nutshell, I sought to work from the inside.

A Journey of Discovery: The 4 As of Manifesting

I went on a journey that was an overhaul to my previous way of living. I did emotional healing, meditated, read self-help books, tried all kinds of therapies, and worked on positive affirmations. I also started to track my external results from having worked internally.

This was when I started to materialize my true dream of abundance. I began to enjoy holistic wellness. From having experienced a positive shift in the state of my being, I decided to become a personal development coach. Soon, I discovered that I was passionate in helping others and discovered a greater sense of purpose.

I manifested a number of miracles that made living fun and more of a breeze. Coins would appear on the floor, desired seats for events, hitting business targets, helpful connections and strangers offering help in obscure places. Through my blog, I attracted a number of opportunities that I never dreamed possible. For one thing, I have been very grateful on being approached as a co-author to this book.

Not all my manifesting experiments turned out successful however. When it came to guessing lottery numbers, for instance, I just could not get the digits in the right order or timing. From the not-so-successful experiments, I would invariably arrive at the same few keys that I have missed out on. To make them easy to remember, I call them the 4As of Manifesting.

1. *Aligning with What You Truly Desire*

Be as authentic as possible. When you are authentic, your desire becomes clear. You are then able to send out clear signals to the Universe. The Universe needs to know what you desire clearly before delivering it to you. It is a process of aligning because it can be the case that you need time to work out what you truly want. You also evolve in tandem during the journey that brings your dream to full bloom.

Many of us face the problem of not being true to our real desires. We delude ourselves into believing that it is something else that we want. For example, it is easy to make the mistake of believing that it is primarily money that we seek. We erroneously think that money can solve all our problems.

For successful manifesting, it helps to connect emotionally with the desired experience of your dream. It is visualizing the experience that money can buy that brings more meaning. It works more powerfully when you are authentic. You are in touch with joy, peace and love continuously.

2. *Practice Non-Attachment to the Outcome of Your Desires*

Manifesting what you want happens more easily when you release your attachment to the outcome of your strong desire, even whilst holding on to your dream. To release yourself from attachment is to feel comfortable with insecurity. You give up your wanting of control over a specific outcome.

Your desires need to be strong to activate the Law of Attraction. Then again, some people are afraid to have desires because they believe that having them creates suffering. It is important to realize that having strong desires alone does not result in suffering. However, it is your attachment to the results of your desires that lead to misery.

When you are attached, you are in the energy of lack. And so you crave. Craving causes suffering because you are never happy with who you are and what you have. By virtue of the Law of Attraction, lack attracts more lack. On the other hand, through *surrendering* to the Universe or God, you acknowledge that there is a higher spiritual order and that you have every bit of trust and belief that things will turn out in the highest good of all concerned.

3. *Focused Attention*

Never lose focus after you have set an intention for your dream. Bear the saying *"energy flows where attention goes"* in mind. You keep the dream alive until it becomes true in your reality.

You are single-minded in your focus. Distraction is the enemy you need to avoid. Your energy becomes diffused when you are unable to concentrate. On the other hand, the greater your focused attention is, the greater your ability to bring your intent into manifestation.

When you practice focused attention, you are being persistent. Persistence is affirming the same intent to the Universe and an indication of your strong desire. No one succeeds without a measure of persistence. That includes Deepak Chopra, Wayne Dyer, and Anthony Robbins; people who lead inspiring lives of abundance.

4. *Take Affirming Action*

Fed on stories of Arabian lamps, wish-granting genies and fairy godmothers, you dream of instant gratification. In your dreams, you prefer to leave hard work out. However, it won't be long before you start to realize that sitting on the couch and trying to apply the Law of Attraction without taking any useful action is not going to work either.

Have you ever heard the saying, *"God helps those who help themselves"*? It cannot be more appropriate to illustrate the necessity of action. Much confusion arises because many people expect instant magic and with no or little effort. What is to know is that while action is necessary, struggle is not. Affirming action puts you in the flow of easy manifesting. Action borne out of conflict and struggle puts you in suffering and exerts unnecessary emotional toil.

Taking action is an affirmation of your belief and trust. You have the belief that your dream is going to come true or that the new idea is worth looking into; and you take action accordingly. So if you have a dream to become the world's best lawyer, then go take the required qualifications. If you have the dream of travelling abroad, read up on where you want to go. If an inspired idea for a business comes, do not sit on it but start planting the seed into the ground.

Living a Dream of Abundance

I now recognize that the pursuit of money will always be a moving target. There is no limit to how much cash reserves, how big a car, how large a home, how many credit cards or how many club memberships I can aspire towards. Discontentment pervaded because I believed that I could only be joyful *when* I attained my dreams. Invariably, I became miserly with myself. I would stop myself from experiencing joy in the meantime because I became overly focused on my not having.

Since working from the inside, I have begun to experience a love for life. I enjoy wonderful connections with everyone around. My relationships with my husband and children have improved tremendously. Work has become a creative expression of who I am. I now live life in greater contentment, connection and celebration.

It's an on-going journey, no doubt. I continue to work towards manifesting the full life I wish to create. With increased consciousness, I am more able to draw on universal support from both seen and unseen forces. Life has become less of a struggle but a flow of synchronistic events that continue to bring my aligned desires into fruition.

About the Author

Evelyn Lim has a strong passion in helping others "master the self in order to manifest a life of abundance". She is an author, adventurer, blogger and life coach from Singapore. She is also a certified Master NLP practitioner, Emotional Freedom Technique practitioner, a Vision Board Counselor and an Intuitive Consultant.

In her book, *"Abundance Alchemy: Journey of Gold"*, Evelyn reveals the secrets for inner alchemy and the keys to living fully. She also shares free but valuable tips for raising abundance consciousness on her website, through content-rich articles and interesting reports.

http://www.AbundanceTapestry.com.

AWAKENING

Tina A. Wake

Rags to riches? Well, that depends on what you call riches. I would say I am an example of riches to riches. I was brought up in a small suburb in New South Wales, Australia, with lots of loving family and friends.

To me, that is richness: *Ample Love.*

Mum and Dad raised me to believe anything is possible. For that I am truly grateful. I believe that you manifest your reality based on your beliefs in yourself: If you don't think you are good enough to attract something, then you either won't attract it, or if you do, it will slip away as fast as it came!

I didn't realise that I was creating my own reality until I was in my mid-twenties though. Until then, I was still fortunate enough that all my dreams had always come true. I just wasn't conscious of the connection between my thoughts and my reality.

After high school, I studied Fashion Design and worked in the industry for a while before deciding to embark on my world travels. So, in my mid-twenties, I set off to teach English in Japan, armed with the words *kimono, karaoke, arigato* and *sushi.*

It was there in Japan, over fifteen years ago, that I met my first ever *guru* who gave me the book 'The Celestine Prophecy'. That book changed my life forever.

With my mother a catholic and my father an atheist, I had always been in religious limbo – neither ever rang true for me, though. Knowing that we are all searching for these kinds of answers, 'The Celestine Prophecy' proved to literally open up my spirituality.

It turned on my 'spiritual tap,' so to speak.

From there I meditated every day and consciously monitored my thoughts. The saying, *'You create your own reality,'* was constantly being thrown around amongst my friends. It was from then on that we all started to take responsibility for every single thing that came up in our lives.

I read and studied whatever I could get my hands on, and as usual, all of my dreams came true. Only this time, I knew why. Now I could start to expand myself knowing that I really was capable of anything.

See, you can be told something until you are blue in the face. Experiencing however is the true understanding. It is then, that what you may have heard a million times, actually makes sense. Otherwise, they are just words.

I was inspired by the works of James Redfield, of course (author of 'The Celestine Prophecy'), Paulo Coehlo, author of 'The Alchemist', Dan Millman, author of 'The Way of The Peaceful Warrior', Neale Donald Walsch, author of the 'Conversations with God' series, and Olivia Newton John.

I believe that every single person is here to uplift those they meet. We are all teachers to each other, if we are open to the messages. Everyone has an innate skill or talent that they may not even realise can help others. It might even be something you have never really thought of as a talent.

Other people say things like, "Wow, it would take me ages to learn to do that, I can't believe you can do it so easily!" or "You are really good at xxxxx". It might be being a good listener, able to help people with their problems, or the ability to organise things to help others clear their mess and find structure in their lives, or the ability to plan and achieve what you set out to do. Trust me, this is a powerful skill. Procrastination is a major barrier for people. It comes up mainly because of fear of failure and of not being good enough.

You might be good at painting, healing, music, or be caring and happy to help others in need. You may be good with your hands for craft or building things, or very friendly and good at connecting people with others. Perhaps you're great at fixing things, or good with technology.

The list goes on.

Not everyone needs to be famous doing what they do. Sometimes the simplest things are the most helpful to others. When you find your talent and passion, watch how quickly the universe adjusts to manifest (or © womanifest, as one of my closest friends always says) your dreams and desires.

I always knew I could sing, write, dance and learn languages. I assumed everyone else could too. It wasn't until I started travelling and meeting a wider range of people, that I soon realised that maybe these things could be my gifts. It made people happy when I sang, and gave me a wonderful connection to unknown worlds when I could communicate in their language. So, when I came back after nearly seven and a half years of travelling around the world, needless to say, I decided it was time to focus on using these talents. While I had started a few of my own fashion labels, I always wanted to write a book as my heart was drawn to writing.

It was any normal day that my life would change again for the better. I had another 'aha' moment that nudged me up to the next notch on my path. I was in the car with my husband at the time, and he asked me a question. When I answered, he laughed using his standard response to my theories, "Not that hippy crap again!"

Now, I also believe that everyone is on their own path – if people don't believe what I believe, then no worries. There are no rules. Our diversity is our beauty.

This time however, I laughed to myself and thought, "If only you knew what I knew. In fact, I wonder what would happen if the whole world knew what I knew?"

Again, I am not claiming to know any more than the next person about spirituality and our place in the universe, however in that exact moment a flash of light like you read about, came in to my head.

The book title 'The Glimpse', movie and all, started playing in my mind. The plot was: at the same instant every single person in the world experienced a Oneness with the Universe. Everyone left their bodies and had a guide who they could ask any question at all, and it would be answered.

When I opened my eyes in that instant, I knew that I would write this book. I suddenly realised that I possessed all of my special traits because I was a messenger.

I don't know if you have ever had an, 'aha' moment, but if you have, you will understand that it is a knowing, almost like a flash in to the future. I could see the book in my hand, and even see myself at the premier opening of the movie, 'The Glimpse'. So, knowing that your thoughts create your own reality, it is with certainty that the book came about. It is with much tried and tested confidence now that I can pass on the ingredients to creating your own reality.

Firstly, you need an idea, or dream.

Secondly, with every cell of your body you need to believe that you can achieve it and that you deserve it. The deserving part may seem inconsequential, but is actually more important than your desire to achieve whatever it is.

Thirdly you need to make a game plan of how you will get to your end goal. It doesn't need to be detailed, but at least have some clue. If you are not good at following through, then at least put it out to the universe that you will be open to those who can lead you to your dream.

Look for signs and take opportunities when they arise.

The sign for me to write my first novel was so clear. It was when I was writing the first that I realised I had even more information to impart. This is when the idea came to me to make it into, 'The Glimpse Trilogy.'

It took me four years to write my first novel. The launching of 'The Glimpse' became a turning point in my life where things fell away that I had grown apart from. Once more positive conditions were in my life, it only took six months each to write the second and third novel.

Fourthly, you must be grateful for your experience. Manifesting is what we do every day of our lives.

What we see around us is literally a mirror of our inner thoughts and beliefs about our place here.

I dream big, and you can too.

So, what is it you want to manifest? What do you think of your current situation? Are you happy with your relationships, both friends, family and sexual? Are you happy with your finances? Your career? Where you live? The list goes on...

And you have created each of these so far, through the power of manifesting what is truly in your heart.

Again, fears of not being worthy for certain things, creates that as a justification to your thoughts over and over. How often do you hear, or even ask yourself, "Why do I keep attracting this or that?" Or, "Why does this always happen to me?"

The answer is simply because you *believe* it will.

The saying, 'I will believe it when I see it,' is actually the wrong way around. It should be, "I will see it when I believe it." There is not enough time to go in to why horrible things happen in this world and why, but if you have time to read 'The Glimpse,' it can explain this in more detail. For now though, we are concentrating on Manifesting.

It is one thing to imagine yourself already jumping around the room winning the lottery, but if deep down you believe in something as simple as, 'you have to work hard to make money,' or the cliché 'Aussie battler' mentality, then it will never materialize. I find that abundance on the financial front is the last layer of onion I need to work on.

I always manifest whatever I need, although until now have not been able to keep it in my hands for as long as I would have liked. I will tell you a funny story though, and things like this happen almost daily to me when I ask the Universe a question.

If you know what signs to look for you will see them everywhere.

I also believe that miracles show you that you are heading in the right direction. Anyway, back to my story.

I had just looked at my bank balance and drove off wondering, "Why haven't I got enough money? I thought I had done everything I could to strip away any negative thoughts pertaining to it? What am I doing wrong?"

I swear no sooner did I think it, than a small truck pulled out in front of me with the company name printed on the side in capital letters, 'LACK Group'.

At first I thought, 'that is not a very good name to have as a company as that is what you are announcing to the world you are.' Then I laughed realising that it actually answered my initial question.

What have I been doing wrong in regards to financial abundance? I have believed in lack. I have believed there isn't enough for everyone. There is though, and since then I have turned those tables.

Now I dream big and encourage others to do so too.

Expand and be all you can be.

Leave a legacy of love in whatever way you can to those you meet; even strangers.

Grow and stretch outside of your comfort zone – the more you learn, the more you realise there is to learn.

I am on the tip of the iceberg now with my spirituality and plan to open some hearts with my Trilogy. If one person learns something positive about themselves from my books, I am grateful.

I love lists. You can follow my progress to see if I truly believe what I set out to do. I hope to inspire you to write a list of your own. This is what I would like to achieve within five years:

1) Become published by a large publishing firm in the USA (Hampton Roads, Hay House or similar).

2) The Glimpse Trilogy to become world famous movies.

3) To write, sing and record the movie soundtracks for each movie.

4) To home school my son, mixing 'traditional' subjects and spiritual ones.

5) Use my fame from my novels and movies to open 'Awake Schooling', a comprehensive alternative education system for those who want to home school their children, incorporating spiritual values.

A way that I have found to work is to write out your goals and dreams, put them in a self-addressed envelope and post them to yourself. Ask your angels for guidance, and be open to the signs they send you.

Following is what I have been saying to myself in my meditations for at least a year, ten times a day, both morning and night:

"I love being the multi-millionaire New York Times best-selling author of The Glimpse Trilogy."

I say it in the present tense as if it is already real, and that I am grateful for it. I imagine helping all of my friends and family achieve their dreams, giving as much as I can to charity, and travelling around the world whenever I like with my family and friends.

Think about what you really want. Write it down. Break it into categories such as Love, Finance, Career, Health or whatever else you want to achieve. You might just want to achieve happiness, but what does that look and feel like to you?

Be clear. The trick of all masters is to keep wishing for the same thing over and over.

It wouldn't help to wish for a great job one day, and then a new house the next, and keep changing your mind. The Universe adjusts to each of your thoughts, so monitor them and keep your dream the same.

Once you achieve it, big or small, expand to the next one.

I wish you good luck on your journey. Life is amazing and I trust you will achieve your dreams. If I can do it, so can you. The world is your oyster, and you are the pearl. Shine your uniqueness like only you can.

About the Author

TINA A. WAKE

Yes that is my real married name. My mother thinks it is hilarious. I was born on the Central Coast, New South Wales, Australia in 1971. I am a Fashion Designer by trade, and left the industry to travel. I lived and worked all over the world for over seven years. I came back and taught both English and Japanese privately, while running a few of my own private fashion labels for a few years.

With a constant interest in and focus on my spiritual growth, I started writing in my spare time. My first novel, 'The Glimpse' was published in 2010. Further titles, Eden and Portals in 'The Glimpse' trilogy were released in August 2011.

I am a stay at home mum to my son Archer, and sing in a 70's and 80's cover band in my spare time.

http://www.theglimpse.com.au

THE LAW OF ATTRACTION LIFESTYLE

Tanja Kraus

Let me set the scene for you. It's about twenty-one degrees, a clear sunny day; possibly one of the most spectacular that Mother Nature has breathed life into, and a light breeze is blowing. It's 11am. I have a café latte in hand from a great coffee shop, and I have eased myself into the morning with a sleep in, a cup of tea, followed by tending to our magnificent horses.

This is pretty much a typical day for me. I don't have a 'j ob' per say and with the exception of a couple obligations, I pretty much do what I want, when I want.

Do I want for more? *Yes.*

Do I have more goals and aspirations? *Yes.*

Do I need it? *No.*

I have a roof, food, a warm bed, and everything else is pretty much my heart's desire. As I settle in to write this chapter on the Law of Attraction, I take a look back at my life to try and understand how I got here.

I wasn't born into money. In fact we were what a lot of people would call poor. We lived basically week-to-week, not that I had much understanding of that as a child. I just knew that when mum opened her wallet to prove she didn't have the five dollars I wanted for something or other, she meant it. That said, we didn't need anything; we were fed, clothed and had a roof over our heads. Though from age eight to eleven, living in a small caravan with two adults and two kids was not cool! We were educated and we had a cat. When I was twelve I got my first horse by convincing my parents it was going to cost less than fifteen dollars per week (sorry mum and dad).

By fourteen I could no longer hide my rebellious streak and at fifteen, I moved out of home with my then boyfriend. By sixteen, I had landed myself a traineeship at a real estate office. Unbeknownst to me this would basically carve out my future. Over the next seven years I led essentially a double life: professional by day and one half of an extremely unhealthy relationship by night. By twenty-two years old I was drained of any remaining self-esteem, as well as my bank accounts. Thirty thousand dollars in debt, with six credit cards, I moved back home.

By now you are probably wondering what on earth my story is doing featured in a book on manifesting, because no one wants to manifest that!

I wanted to share the background with you, so you know that no matter where you came from, *changing your life is possible*. You can attract amazing things into your life and you can achieve greatness. It took me a long time to realise that it doesn't matter where you came from, what you were told as a child, or where you are in your life right now. All that matters is how much you want it and how much you believe you can get it. That is the common denominator in all of the Law of Attraction stories that you hear.

When Jim Carrey wrote himself a cheque for millions of dollars when he was broke, he knew he wanted to be a hugely successful actor. When Edison failed his 1000th invention, he knew he was one step closer to success, and when Katie Holmes had posters on her wall of Tom Cruise, she knew she wanted to marry him. We hear the celebrity Law of Attraction stories because, well, they're celebrities. There are millions of success stories around the globe and you could be one of them!

I didn't know what the Law of Attraction was until about twelve months ago. Up until then I was just 'winging it'. From the time I was a child I knew that I was going to be rich and successful, or a combination of the two. This was a continuous thought through everything and to this day it always remains my mindset. Even when I had to eat onion sandwiches for dinner because I had no food, I knew that things would change. Looking back even further, when I was competing on my horse, I would humbly say out loud, "Oh I won't win", but secretly I could see my horse with that blue ribbon around his neck.

I guess this was my first exposure to the Law of Attraction.

2001 was the first year I actually wrote down my goals. The biggest one was to buy a house, which I did, thirty thousand dollars in debt. Over the next ten years I achieved some pretty awesome things. I invested in more property and purchased the real estate agency that I worked for, becoming one of the youngest licensee/principals in Australia. I continued my study with horses, which in turn led me to the loving, healthy, happy, fun relationship I am in now. I bought my dream car, and sold the real estate office for a record-breaking price. I moved to what I call 'paradise on earth', and my first book was published; the list goes on.

I will be the first to admit that there were some bumps and challenges along the way. It's not all a drive on easy street. All this I achieved without even knowing what the Law of Attraction was. I just wrote down the goals and kept a mental picture in my mind.

Late in 2010 I decided that I wanted 2011 to be an awesome year across many facets of my life. After making that decision, I was in a bookstore for the signing and promotion of my book, and I purchased a book called 'The Power of Influence' by Sarah Prout. I read it, loved it and logged onto her website. I don't really know why, but I did. On there, I found that there was an opportunity to join an online course called Adventures in Manifesting. With less than 24 hours before the close of the course, I hit the 'Buy Now' button (little did I know there would be a free revision of the course months later!). To this day I can't explain why, I didn't really even know what the course was about, but something drew me to it. The sixteen-week course is now at a close, but the achievements made by participants were grand. For me learning about the Law of Attraction philosophies has opened up an entire realm of new possibilities.

2011 is shaping up to be awesome! I have two more books due out this year, and I have made a dramatic shift onto a new career path, a career that I have wanted since I was a teenager. For me the Law of Attraction is a lifestyle. It is not something you do for an hour a day. Rather it is an attitude you have all day, every day. For some readers it may seem that it is all about material things, however it is so much more than that. I am calmer, more centered, focused and engaged in the now than I have been in a long, long time. Sometimes I wonder why I didn't discover this a lot sooner, maybe life would have been a little easier. Perhaps I wasn't ready. Maybe if it had come sooner, in my infinite wisdom, I may have thought it was a load of hogwash.

You may be wondering now, where do I start? Well, you start at the beginning.

The first step is, believing you can. The second step, knowing what it is that you want in your life and the third step, writing it down.

No matter how far-fetched it may seem, write it down. The more specific you can be the better. For example, instead of 'I want to write a book', write down 'I want to write, and have published, a children's book that helps kids improve their self-esteem'. Instead of 'I want a bigger house', write down 'I want a house with five bedrooms so each of our kids can have their own room, and our friends and family can come to stay'.

The best and simplest Law of Attraction example I have heard is about cars. When you decide to buy a new car, or you go and buy one and you know the make and model, you start seeing them everywhere. This is your subconscious mind bringing to the attention of your conscious mind what you want. It's yelling at you, 'Look! That's what you want! Look, there is another one!'

Tell your mind what you want, and it will bring to your attention the opportunities you need to get it.

When I first started the Adventures in Manifesting course, I wanted more exposure for my book and myself. Now I have been a guest blogger on two different websites, have two permanent guest spots on other websites, and I am featured in this book with not only some of my idols but some of the most recognizable people in the world!

Wow! If that isn't exposure, I don't know what is.

I truly believe that if you are reading this book, you have attracted it into your life somehow, because you are ready. Or if you are already an avid Law of Attraction believer, maybe one of the authors will resonate with you. I hope you do with the opportunity what is possible.

About the Author

Tanja Kraus is a focused and passionate entrepreneur. Living 'the dream' in a coastal town of New South Wales, Australia, Tanja is a successful property investor, Author of Maximum Returns, Minimum Concerns – A Guide to Successful Property Investment, business coach and horse breeder / trainer.

Tanja is currently working on another 2 exciting book projects, due to hit the stands in late 2011, and is passionate about building esteem and inspiring women and teen girls to embrace a 'what are you waiting for' attitude to life. Tanja's full story and information on all of her projects can be found at her website.

http://www.tanjakraus.com

STORIESELLING

Michael Firth

As I write these words I must say that, on one level, consciously it's really hard to believe that I'm actually writing this story about my journey of manifestation over the last few years. Having said that, on another level, subconsciously it all makes perfect sense, because everything you are about to read was written down and well planned for within my goals a little over four years ago.

To ensure you gain some real clarity around my story, I will have to take you back ten years: back to the time when I was newly divorced, a single dad with a two year old toddler and a one year old baby.

Having halved my income overnight because of a business collapse, and having a major career change due to way too much mental pressure, times were certainly tough. My life seemed to have collapsed around me, and I hated who I had become when I looked in the mirror due to things I had done in the past. Most importantly though, I had finally decided to begin to face the mental issues that had been swept under the carpet due to sexual abuse that occurred in my childhood over thirty-three years earlier.

Aside from addressing where I was mentally at the time, no matter how hard I worked after my divorce and tried to get ahead, there just didn't seem to be any light at the end of the tunnel; the financial hole I was in just seemed to get deeper and deeper.

For a number of years I worked really hard in my role as a Business Development Manager in the mortgage industry. At the same time I jumped unknowingly from one dysfunctional relationship into another. All the while I did my utmost to become the best dad I could be, as my number one priority was my kids as they grew up.

I craved to dig myself out of the hole I created for myself, and wondered if I was ever going to get on the right track with anything at all; business, relationships, finances or even life in general.

Then just over four years ago it happened. One of my good friends Barry Hester telephoned me and invited me to attend a workshop he was presenting called 'The Goal Achiever' by Bob Proctor. He had purchased the license to present it in Victoria, Australia, and since I had always been open to personal development, I agreed to attend and committed to participate with every ounce of mental energy I could muster. During the course he drilled into so much detail about goal setting that we all spent an entire day writing down what we wanted out of life. We looked at the reasons that most people like me had eluded massive success in life for so long, and he gave us some simple strategies that absolutely everyone could apply.

I distinctly remember that I came out of that day with a large list of what I wanted to achieve in my life, but more importantly I came out with a laser focus of all my biggest burning desires in life, along with definitive time frames and priorities of when I would achieve them.

I had always thought I was an avid goal setter, but what I realized during the course of this day was that I had always been too wishy-washy; I had no real clarity of priorities and never reviewed my goals regularly enough to have any real impact. One of the major points that was discussed at length during the course kept running over and over in my mind:

You don't need to know *how* you are going to achieve all of your goals when you get started.

The magic was just in writing them down to start with, then repeating them out loud to yourself over and over each and every day, followed by massive action.

I wrote down my goals, made plans for their achievement, and watched movies like 'The Secret' over and over. I installed two vision boards in the house and encouraged the kiddies to get involved too. The small card that I wrote my goals down on that day during the course stated the following three points, in a paragraph written as if they had already been achieved:

I am a professional public speaker, traveling the world.

I have a six figure passive income from a network marketing business.

I *have* increased my total income from all sources by seven times.

Just two weeks after the course had been run, to my surprise, Barry called me and asked if I would like to assist him in co-presenting the next course. To say this made my day would have been a major understatement. It sat perfectly within my goals as a stepping-stone for the future, although as you will soon find out, this proved to be just the start of the magic that was to come.

Six months later the CEO and the founding Director of the company I had been working with as a Business Development Manager for many years asked me if I would be open to taking on a new position they felt I was quite well suited for. The position was to be called the National Sales Coach, looking after a few thousand individual mortgage brokers across Australia and New Zealand, along with another friend and colleague of mine, Gail from Sydney, Australia, who would be sharing the responsibility.

I nearly wet my pants at the thought of it.

It was just the lucky break I was looking for: a chance to make my mark on the industry and gain more exposure for future plans to work for myself. Was it a coincidence or did it result from my focused goal setting, visualization and action? Gail and I took the role and grabbed it with both hands, whilst we literally created our own concepts from scratch from the many years of experience we had accrued between us.

During this time I felt it was really important for me to invest in myself and get some more guidance and mentoring if I was to excel in this field. I had always believed in having a coach and had worked with various coaches and mentors though the years, so I commissioned the services of a speaker coach by the name of Pete Crofts from the 'Humourversity' in Melbourne, Australia. Pete was well known for his public speaking coaching with a humorous twist, as well as his expertise in guiding new speakers to establishing themselves in the marketplace. Pete became a great mentor of mine for about 3 years of my journey and assisted to get me ready to launch out on my own. I used to think of him as 'Yoda the wise one' because of the profound nature of some of his advice. He also reminded me of a lighthouse that could see all of the icebergs in my path that I was unaware of and that would later contribute to some of my success.

Simultaneously, as I was establishing myself in this new role as a speaker within the mortgage industry, a good friend of mine Marcus suggested we take on a new challenge with a new company which was about to enter Australia. I had met Marcus along the way whilst I was dabbling in one or two network marketing companies.

How could I possibly take on more?! I was flying on planes around Australia and New Zealand each week, juggling my responsibilities with the kids, as well as my public speaking role. I said to him, "Do you have any idea how busy I am? You must be mad!" He then proceeded to explain to me that I would be able to stay at home with the kiddies and build the business in my spare time due to the online web cast technology they were using. Once again, this seemed like just the lucky break I was looking for. I knew that as a single dad, I just wouldn't have time to build a network marketing business in the old fashioned way, traveling all over the place whilst keeping up with work as well!

By this time it became very evident to me that the more I read my goals out loud, visualized my success, reviewed my progress and stayed focused, the more positive magic seemed to happen.

It's also worth pointing out that the journey wasn't all smooth sailing. For example the global financial crisis kicked in just after my national role started in the mortgage industry. This resulted in the company downsizing and eliminating the other National Sales Coach, leaving me with the complete responsibility and added pressure of the role all on my own. Additionally, with very little time to contribute to a relationship, whilst admittedly in a half-hearted way, I tried to find the right lady for myself and the kids – only to end up with a broken heart due to a partner cheating behind my back.

So why do I tell you all of this? Well sometimes I find that some people use the story of their past as an excuse not to soldier on, or as a reason for their lack of success. My advice is that you just need to *learn* from the experience, dust yourself off and get back on the horse. You can succeed again, and you can love again. In fact, success in anything is rarely a dead straight journey to the top.

In effect what I'm saying is that despite what life throws at us, we all need to take control of the *stories* we are selling ourselves on a daily basis. If we find that we are entertaining negative or destructive thinking, we need to become 'The Mind Police' and handcuff that thinking and banish it from our minds forever.

So where is my life right now as we close out this chapter of 'StorieSelling'?

Well, I left the corporate world and went out on my own as professional speaker, forming the company 'StorieSelling' in 2010. I'm proud to say 'StorieSelling' now has speaking engagements booked left, right and centre. I am earning *double* what I did when I worked for a boss in *half* the time, and have never looked back.

I am on the Australian advisory board for an international network marketing business owned by some of the richest names worldwide in television commercials. I have also just toppled into an additional passive six figure income as a result, just as I had written down on my goal card. My income hasn't quite reached the complete goal of seven times what I was earning yet, but the opportunities that are falling into my lap each and every day now give me 100% confidence that this day will come to pass in the not too distant future; although I must point out that my income is certainly *very* healthy now and the five year goal hasn't yet reached its deadline.

Due to the freedom that these two goals have given me, I now have more time to dedicate to giving back to the community, which is an ongoing process of development and growth for me. These days I like to use my speaking gift in more creative ways to raise money for charity; and you guessed it – the very first project that I embarked upon once I left my job was to speak to businesses to raise money for a charity that would help kids like me, who were victims of sexual abuse.

Though I would have to say that last achievement is one of the most soul fulfilling benefits of my journey so far, there is one last outcome that has had an enormous impact on me, which I would love to finish this chapter on for all the softies out there.

If you doubt writing down your goals and being very clear about what you are after, then consider this: All the way through this journey so far you will note that I was certainly laser focused on my business achievements and looking after my kids. However, although I wrote it down, I never read regularly any goals relating to relationships. Well let me say now, just seven months ago, knowing that all of my business goals were right on track, I told all of my close friends that I should start to get serious about this part of my life. I wrote down exactly what I wanted and got ready to embark on that part of the journey...

Two months later, like a present handpicked just for me, I met the most amazing, big hearted woman I have ever had the pleasure to know. Not only is she stunningly gorgeous and a beautiful person too, but her wish list of a man just happened to be every single thing that I stand for in life too.

So if there were one thought and gift I could leave you with, it would be this:

Spend time creating your wish list of all the things you want to be, do and have in your lifetime. Condense this down to a paragraph about your life and the way it will be when you have achieved these dreams. Read them daily as if you have already achieved them and embark on massive action with faith that the world will create an amazing life for you. My journey just keeps getting better and better, and I know yours will too.

About the Author

After leaving school at a very young age and initially training as an apprentice electrician, Michael moved into the sales profession just after his 19th birthday. With more than twenty years experience in sales, he has worked with companies such as Yellow Pages, Drake International and Citibank just to name a few.

Over the past 8 years, Michael worked with PLAN Australia in the business development team and later progressed to become the National Sales Coach working with over 2000 mortgage brokers across Australia and New Zealand.

Additionally Michael has over 14 years of public speaking and coaching experience which was obtained through his involvement at various leadership levels within the network marketing industry, both in Australia and overseas.

Michael's expertise and speciality is creating and presenting passionate action packed seminars and training events both live and online.

To assist you in keeping on track with your journey of manifestation please visit his website (2).

http://www.storieselling.com.au

http://www.themindpolice.com (2)

THE POWER OF POSITIVE SELF-TALK

Brian Tracy

Perhaps the most powerful influence on your attitude and personality is what you say to yourself, and believe. It is not what happens to you, but how you respond internally to what happens to you, that determines your thoughts and feelings and, ultimately, your actions. By controlling your inner dialogue, or "self-talk," you can begin to assert control over every other dimension of your life.

What is Self-Talk?

Your self-talk—the words that you use to describe what is happening to you, and to discuss how you feel about external events—determines the quality and tone of your emotional life. When you see things positively and constructively and look for the good in each situation and each person, you have a tendency to remain naturally positive and optimistic. Since the quality of your life is determined by how you feel, moment to moment, one of your most important goals should be to use every psychological technique available to keep yourself thinking about what you want and to keep your mind off of what you don't want, or what you fear.

The Inevitable Truth

You are continually faced with challenges and difficulties, with problems and disappointments, with temporary setbacks and defeats. They are an unavoidable and inevitable part of being human. But, as you draw upon your resources to respond effectively to each challenge, you grow and become a stronger and better person. In fact, without those setbacks, you could not have learned what you needed to know and developed the qualities of your character to where they are today.

Reaction

Much of your ability to succeed comes from the way you deal with life. One of the characteristics of superior men and women is that they recognize the inevitability of temporary disappointments and defeats, and they accept them as a normal and natural part of life. They do everything possible to avoid problems, but when problems come, superior people learn from them, rise above them, and continue onward in the direction of their dreams.

There is a natural tendency in all of us to react emotionally when our expectations are frustrated in any way. When something we wanted and hoped for fails to materialize, we feel a temporary sense of disappointment and unhappiness. We feel disillusioned. We react as though we have been punched in the "emotional solar plexus".

The optimistic person, however, soon moves beyond this disappointment. He responds quickly to the adverse event and interprets it as being temporary, specific and external to himself. The optimist takes full control of his inner dialogue and counters the negative feelings by immediately reframing the event so that it appear positive in some way.

Positive Thinking

Since your conscious mind can hold only one thought at a time, either positive or negative, if you deliberately choose a positive thought to dwell upon, you keep your mind optimistic and your emotions positive. Since your thoughts and feelings determine your actions, you will tend to be a more constructive person, and you will move much more rapidly toward the goals that you have chosen.

It all comes down to the way you talk to yourself on a regular basis. In our courses of problem solving and decisions making, we encourage people to respond to problems by changing their language from negative to positive. Instead of using the word *problem*, we encourage people to use the word *situation*. You see, a problem is something that you deal with. The event is the same. It's the way you interpret the event to yourself that makes it sound and appear completely different.

The Superior Person

The hallmark of the fully mature, fully functioning, self-actualizing personality is the ability to be objective and unemotional when caught up in the inevitable storms of daily life. The superior person has the ability to continue talking to himself in a positive and optimistic way, keeping his mind calm, clear and completely under control. The mature personality is more relaxed and aware and capable of interpreting events more realistically and less emotionally than is the immature personality. As a result, the mature person exerts a far greater sense of control and influence over his environment, and is far less likely to be angry, upset, or distracted.

The starting point in the process of becoming a highly effective person is to monitor and control your self-talk every minute of the day. Keep your thoughts and your words positive and consistent with your goals, and keep your mind focused on what you want to do and the person you want to be.

Action Strategies:

Here are five ideas you can use to help you to be a more positive and optimistic person:

First: Resolve in advance that no matter what happens, you will not allow it to get you down. You will respond in a constructive way. You will take a deep breath, relax and look for whatever good the situation may contain. When you make this decision in advance, you mentally prepare yourself so that you are not knocked off balance when things go wrong, as they inevitably will.

Second: Neutralize any negative thoughts or emotions by speaking to yourself positively all the time. Say things like, "I feel healthy! I feel happy! I feel terrific!" As you go about your job, say to yourself, I like myself, and I love my work!" Say things like, "Today is a great day; it's wonderful to be alive!" According to the law of expression, whatever is expressed is impressed. Whatever you say to yourself or others is impressed deeply into your subconscious mind and is likely to become a permanent part of your personality.

Third: Look upon the inevitable setbacks that you face as being temporary, specific and external. View the negative situations as a single event that is not connected to other potential events and that is caused largely by external factors over which you can have little control. Simply refuse to see the event as being in any way permanent, pervasive or indicative of personal incompetence of inability.

Fourth: Remember that it is impossible to learn and grow and become a successful person without adversity and difficulties. You must contend with and rise above them in order to become a better person. Welcome each difficulty by saying, "That's good!" and then look into the situation to find the good in it.

Fifth: Keep your thoughts on your goals and dreams, on the person you are working toward becoming. When things go wrong temporarily, respond by saying to yourself, "I believe in the perfect outcome of every situation in my life." Resolve to be cheerful and pleasant, and resist every temptation toward negativity and disappointment. View a disappointment as an opportunity to grow stronger and talk about it to yourself and others in a positive and optimistic way.

When you practice positive self-talk, and keep your words and your mental pictures consistent with your goals and dreams, there is nothing that can stop you from being the success you are meant to be.

About the Author

Brian Tracy is one of America's most respected authorities on developing organizational and human potential. His insights in to leadership, personal effectiveness, and business strategy, which he presents to more than half a million people around the world each year in his talks and seminars, produce immediate changes and long-term results.

His experience in business, combined with his wonderful ability to inform, entertain, inspire and motivate audiences, makes him one of the top business speakers and trainers in the world today. For more information, please visit:

http://www.briantracy.com

THE POWER OF GUIDANCE

Rebecca Anne LoCicero

Have you ever been in the center of your own life transition and didn't even realize it? I have seen many times people go from one step to another without recognizing how perfectly placed each step they took was toward exactly what they wanted.

I remember sitting within a cubicle area, in a large office building, answering phones and hitting the same buttons day after day. All the while I was thinking, am I in the right place? When did my desire to make a difference in the world start to fade away? I sat back in my rolling office chair and thought about where I was and what brought me there.

As a divorced single mom looking to make ends meet, I thought I was lucky to find a job that paid ok and kept my life functioning at the norm society thought it should. However, I felt frustrated, unproductive, misdirected and, most of all, ready for a change.

I just didn't believe it could happen.

Before this point of surrendering to survive, you could find my focus on the New Age world, psychic information, mediumship, intuition, energy healing and anything else along that line. I was newly exploring my full awareness of the intuitive ability I strongly possessed, and just beginning to learn and understand soul connections to the Universe. Meanwhile, I was immersing myself in sharing my gift of knowledge and healing through psychic readings and more.

When reality stepped in and life presented me with obstacles though, I retreated. I started feeling uneducated, naïve, and was swimming in the pit of denial. There was fear: was I capable of moving from the mundane job that was supporting us into a risky yet profoundly purposeful line of work?

I took a leap of faith and decided to literally focus on manifestation. Specifically I decided to manifest guidance! I just knew as I sat straight up in that office chair, pushing buttons as if there was more to life, that if there was a way to break free, I would get a sign! That same day someone posted on their cubicle wall:

"Men often become what they believe themselves to be. If I believe I cannot do something, it makes me incapable of doing it. But when I believe I can, then I acquire the ability to do it even if I didn't have it in the beginning."
Mahatma Gandhi.

My soul leaped for joy when I acknowledged that statement as a sign!

Step 1: Have Faith (the first step to manifestation).

If you cannot have faith that something is going to happen, then it won't. For me at that moment faith was accepting that there was a path to a new career. This path had to have a new focus, and along with that came the faith that what I needed to do would present itself to me. So I said out loud, "Ok God, bring on the guidance."

Once you have faith you can create any path, and you don't have to do it alone.

Manifesting guidance was what I wanted to do. Now I just had to figure out how to do that. You do not always have to hit the wall to turn around; sometimes it is done for you. Manifestation becomes the reflection of what your true inner soul desire is calling out for. They say, 'be careful what you ask for' and I knew that my soul wanted to escape the confines of the cubicle and move out into the world.

My first 'aha' moment was from one of Oprah's episodes about making lists. That was it, writing my list of what I wanted in my life! Quickly and clearly I listed what I wanted, with a little note on the bottom that said "I am willing to accept what may come without looking for perfection, Amen."

1. I want out of my job.

2. I want to work as a psychic medium.

3. I want a new car.

4. Another 'want' and so on…

The next morning (#1 & #2.) I was relieved of my position for being too perceptive and too friendly with the clients and their needs. They felt that I was always two steps ahead of the process and that was in turn confusing the clients.

Really? I was fired for being intuitive and nice?!

There was no way to deny that I was being shown the power of manifesting my life into the direction I requested. It was my actions that lead me to **be let go** from a job for doing what I wanted to do in the first place. I just smiled and laughed at myself! Was it possible? Manifestation was something I had disregarded for so long and now I was about to dive into the reality of *purposeful* attraction.

Step 2: Acknowledge.

I drove home that day with thankful prayers on my lips for being released of that cubicle area. I could no longer deny that with faith and conscious direction toward a goal, manifestation can occur. I had no other option than to acknowledge that it had really happened.

In order to accept it as a manifested sign, I had to first acknowledge that it happened and was purposeful. I can say it was life changing for sure – without a 9-5 in my way I was ready to face my gifts and abilities as a psychic medium and present them to my outside world. My deep belief was that God does not ask you to do anything that you are not already ready to do.

Of course I also realized that I needed to adjust my manifestation list right away.

Step 3: Acceptance.

Truthfully, accepting and defining who I was to myself was harder than conveying that identity to the outside world. I started to regain the connections to the metaphysical community. I was able to see that there were great opportunities and there was nothing to stop me, except myself! There was no easy road that I could see yet, but there was that desire for perseverance. All I could hear was 'get organized', 'make a list', and 'set a goal'. These were all concepts I had done before yet I still had doubt.

I was jealous of those who were doing the work I wanted to do and I felt judgmental. Once I got honest with myself though, I realized that this was a clear reflection of my fear:

I was afraid to succeed.

Instead I was embracing my refusal to acknowledge and accept that I could do whatever I set my heart and mind to do. I had learned from many that you need to have the business side of things all in order, so there were websites, business cards and flyers put in place. But I still felt unguided. Then I remembered a mantra I was brought up with.

"God helps those who help themselves." Ben Franklin.

So my newly edited list included my desire to manifest more precise guidance. I asked for specific books, helpful connections, inspiring mentors and certified educational resources. One after another crossed my path and each was a gift that I was able to recognize as a manifested resource. It was the guidance that I needed to manifest to produce what I wanted.

I actually had to practice being aware and honest with myself with each sign.

One great gift of guidance came from the daycare parking lot. While backing out I was waved down by another mom who was running over to my car with a large box in her hands. "I have cassettes for you" she said. I stopped and greeted her as she handed me a box full of books on tape. I wondered how she knew my old Volvo still had a tape player.

"I heard that you're a psychic. These are a bunch of spiritual books I thought you would enjoy." With much thanks and a little conversation about how she overheard what I did for work, I put the box in the car and ventured home.

There were over thirty books on tape from 'The Four Noble Truths' to John Edwards to Edgar Cayce. My favorite was 'Wisdom of the Masters' by Dr. Wayne Dyer. When he read Rumi's 'Chickpea to Cook,' ancient wisdom vibrated through me and has had a lasting effect.

There were many acknowledgeable signs from my list. Books by great authors such as Caroline Myss, who brought me great understanding to the complexity I always assumed existed within the soul/spirit/mind and body connection. Manifesting guidance is still an active part of my daily prayers.

You should always be open to accepting new ideas and concepts; the learning mind is a growing soul.

The most profound experiences came from the divine connections to the spiritual realm around my personal soul. The guidance being sent to me, through God and all the other entities beyond became a natural part of the process to manifest in my life what I knew as the next steps.

There is still a never-ending flow of mentors and each one perfect. This is the same with the endless opportunities to expand your education. You can take classes, groups, programs and more in every corner of the globe on any topic you desire! There is no limit to being guided to learn something new. You advance your soul in a way that allows there to be a deeper understanding of what possibilities are out there to manifest.

Everyone I came across became a resource of inspiration. Every idea I had became another opportunity to grow in the metaphysical field I was now actively working within. Clients were coming to receive accurate and joy filled messages whenever my schedule was open, and the worry over being able to support my family financially was no longer a stressor in my life. With all this manifesting, I found myself growing leaps and bounds within the New Age community, and accepted I could manifest the information to persevere.

The concept of a coincidence forever vanished. If at any time I was within confusion on where to go next or what path to consider, I could always rely on the faith I had to manifest the right guidance to help me along the way.

Eventually you will find that your soul's experiences become a part of the manifestation for others as you share your knowledge and awareness.

While preparing to present to a group of one hundred, I was asked by another medium what kind of classes I taught. "Teach? Not me" I said. Although I loved the idea, I found myself again placing fear ahead of the possibility. "I wouldn't know how to begin to teach what I know, and I am not an expert" was my response. Little did I know I had just manifested another opportunity to grow within my work. This medium responded to me with a simple guided statement:

"A teacher teaches best what they need to learn most".

It is amazing how, at that second, I knew I would teach and mentor. I later learned the author of that quote was Richard David Bach, an American author who also stated:

"Argue for your limitations and sure enough they're yours".

I was not willing to have limitations. I was no longer against any wall of judgment, jealousy or fear.

I was open.

Have the ability to say 'yes' to something that comes your way! The opportunities you come across are those that you have manifested through your soul's divine connection to what life can offer you.

Make a list! Use a paper and pen and put those thoughts down if it helps. Just make a conscious note of what you would like. Look for the clear path that feels right and look for confirmation. We are all placed perfectly where we are supposed to be at each moment. Where will your moment take you? Dr. Dyer also stated:

"You have everything you need for complete peace and total happiness right now."

I am ready for it all, excited to experience life, and full of joy. I know where I have been and feel that with faith and focused manifestation you can find all the guidance you need.

Take action, pay attention and accept that you can bring into your life the experiences, encounters and people that are perfect for your path. Acknowledge and be aware of the guidance being shown to you. Define what you would like to have and accept that it may not come perfectly, but will be in complete harmony with your soul.

About the Author

Rebecca Anne LoCicero embraces her natural ability to communicate with the spiritual realm and views this gift as a blessing from God. Since 1994 she has been working as a Psychic Medium while guiding and teaching others to awaken and acknowledge their own intuitive soul. She has been experiencing connections with souls who have crossed as well as receiving messages and guidance from the highest divine resources since a very young age. As an author, Rebecca Anne shares her story and viewpoints through her first book, 'Living with Messages from Heaven, An advocate for psychic mediumship & prophets in the millennium'. She appears as the illustrator in her second book, 'I AM THE BEYOND', written by Janine Baryza-Ly; Janine & Rebecca Anne together host the humorous stage show 'Comedy from Beyond' as well as host a weekly radio show.

As co-founder of 'The Beyond Center' in Connecticut (www.TheBeyondCenter.com), Rebecca Anne has the opportunity to share her services. Worldwide, nationwide or locally, her goal is to bring humanity spiritual enlightenment with love and compassion, while empowering all to discover and identify their own sacred connections.

http://www.Rebeccaanne.org

LETTING GO OF JUDGMENT
TO ATTRACT WHAT MATTERS

Carolyn Hidalgo

If I could share the magical ingredients that have allowed me to manifest my heart's desires, it would be learning to *trust* myself, *letting go* of judgment, and stepping into *'being'*.

I was all about 'doing' my life. I grew up in a loving environment where working hard and accomplishing things was part of my DNA. When I meet people today, they laugh when I tell them I used to be a chartered accountant – a part of my life where I now feel completely disconnected. I only knew how to think analytically, with a skeptical mind, and search for answers with the need for external proof. Following a genuine interest in understanding people, I completed a specialist program in psychology, but graduated with a Bachelor of commerce degree. My social programming led me to fear that I would never get a 'real' job pursuing psychology.

Having a respected profession that secured financial independence was a strong belief I had growing up. It wasn't *wrong*, and I have no regrets, but I wasn't aware that so many of the choices I was making had been influenced by belief systems that were not necessarily my own.

As a stay at home mom with twin girls who had just turned 2, and my son nearly 4, life was a blur. My husband worked long hours: gone before the kids were up, and home after they went to sleep. My belief system was that the house and kids were 100% my responsibility. My mom, a physician, had successfully raised six of us born within nine years, while my dad completed his surgical training that led to long hours growing a busy practice in orthopedics. How hard could this be?

It was 2003, and I became curious when a friend told me that four other women had been meeting a life coach for the past ten years. Wanting to create her own group, my friend asked if I would be interested in joining. "I'll go to the first meeting to find out what life coaching is, but I have no time to join a group," I thought.

To my surprise, that first meeting completely changed the direction of my life: I decided not to return to my career as a financial executive, and became a professional life coach.

I began to discover how my social programming limited the way I was seeing the world, and that what I really needed was to break out of my box and get out of my own way.

I didn't realize how much I had been living on the surface of my life. In my mind, I had it all: a loving husband, 3 beautiful, happy, healthy children, and such laughter and harmony amongst my growing extended family (including my in-laws!) that left me feeling truly blessed.

What we shared at that first life coaching meeting opened up something I was unknowingly yearning for: to live my life with more depth, meaning, and purpose. We discussed the bigger vision for our lives and for our children that no one really talks about. We were all so darn busy! Who has time to stop and think about what really matters?

> – *Reflect on your own values. What do you long for? What makes your heart sing, lights you up, and makes time fly by? What fulfills your deepest desires? Who inspires you? What difference do you want to make in the world? What do you believe is your purpose for being here? What are you willing to stand up for in your life, even when it goes against social norms and expectations?*

What we see includes so much of what we cannot see...

We unknowingly fill in the gaps with judgments, expectations, and assumptions. We see the world not *as it is*, but *as we are*. We operate with limited vision, holding one perspective of what we believe is 'right'... And that can keep us stuck. It is difficult to judge when you are in a state of being open, curious, and having that delicious sense of wonder that we witness in our children.

As young children we learn to wear social masks, fear what others think, and desire to meet other's approval and expectations. Judgment has us view the world in terms of 'right' or 'wrong'; polar opposites that miss all the possibilities in between. We condemn or praise before we can see the whole picture, and fill in the gaps with thinking that is limited to our existing programmed beliefs. Artificially, we feel 'good' or 'bad', and don't question whether we are holding integrity with what we value in our lives.

When we let go of judgment, true emotions flow positively, we feel more at peace, and become attuned to the things that show up in life that resonate.

This is the doorway to manifesting your desires.

When we attach ourselves to a need to be 'right' (self-righteousness) we automatically make others 'wrong', and end up feeling anxiety and anger as we attempt to fix, correct, and change others. We only have the power to change ourselves.

Our egos have us living in fear, where judgment, selfishness, greed, and insecurity serve as a block to manifesting our desires. These low vibration emotions keep us in a state that prevents us from attracting what we want, which includes the higher vibrations of joy, excitement, and love. Like attracts like.

My story was all about establishing security through a loving husband, financial independence, acquiring knowledge, playing by the rules, fulfilling others' expectations, being productive, and respected. I was living neither in fear, nor love – just content with life on what felt like a straight line.

There was nothing wrong with any of this, but I couldn't see how my social programming had limited the choices available to me. I processed everything analytically with an outward focus instead of internally with my heart's emotion and spirit living integrally with my own truth. I didn't know what I didn't know.

When you can let go of the judgmental thinking of 'right' and 'wrong', you can begin to trust yourself, have true faith and hope in what's infinitely possible to create in your life.

> – *Stay open, curious, and notice what resonates emotionally and spiritually. Then, move into action – even when it seems impossible! You will feel fear and discomfort because you are letting go of your social programming – trust and go.*

Have you ever found yourself saying or doing things because you felt a need to meet other people's expectations? How about to avoid conflict or maintain harmony, even though it's not what you really want? What if I told you there is a way to have both?

When we let go of criticism and judgment, and shift over to a place of true compassion and kindness, seeing ourselves as human beings all connected doing the best we can, an opening is created.

Your authentic light will reveal itself as you let go of the limiting beliefs of social programming that run your story. Judgment, criticism, and having an opinion are often confused. We all have our own opinions or ways we see the world. Truth is in the eye of the beholder. When we run across others whose 'truth' conflicts with our own, we often end up criticizing or judging. There is a difference though between judging things, and judging people.

We want to make decisions that serve our best interest and look to find a 'right' answer. Should I take this course? Marry this person? This is simply choosing between 'things' …

However, when we judge people, including ourselves, we create an obstacle to letting our own light shine, and prevent others from showing up fully. We learn to condemn and feel contempt for others. It begins as a child when we are told, "you are 'good' or 'bad', and 'right' or 'wrong'". Many of us are holding onto judgmental thoughts of not being good enough on some level. Limiting beliefs are really judgments of the way we think we 'should be'.

– *Begin to notice when you use the word 'should' towards yourself and others. Ask yourself whether you are criticizing or judging, as opposed to discerning the truth, and focusing on the values you choose to hold that you want to grow into.*

When the documentary 'The Secret' came out in 2006, introducing the concept of the Law of Attraction, I was already stepping out of my box and letting go of limiting beliefs I had of what is 'right' and 'wrong'. For me, 'The Secret' was not so much about manifesting desires as it was about opening up to a broader perspective that gave me a glimpse of Universal principles. I suddenly found myself on a spiritual quest for my own truth and began to devour books on quantum physics and spirituality.

One of my girlfriends hired an angel reader for a group of us to try something that sounded like fun. I was skeptical, but my curiosity was sparked and I sat in amazement as this angel reader shared things about my life that were impossible for her to know. It confirmed there was so much in the Universe that I simply wasn't aware of. She also told me, 'You will be moving this year.' Within a month, I walked into a home for sale my sister-in-law and friend encouraged me to see. As I walked through each room, it was like ticking off a checklist of everything I wanted in my next home. It was completely out of our price range though ... or so I thought.

This friend turned out to be a budding real estate guru, and within a few short months of watching 'The Secret', I was living in my dream home. I realized that what 'The Secret' was teaching, I had just pulled off.

How did I do that?

I looked back and realized I had thoughts of what I wanted in my next house even though I had not written it down, created a vision board or even told any friends. My thoughts sounded like, "It would be nice in my next house when I have..." While I always felt grateful and really enjoyed my previous home, it was as if I had been making silent wishes over time and *poof*, they all appeared.

Coincidences and signs, including the 11:11 prompt I had seen as a child were now appearing everywhere, along with a meaning I now understand for my own life. My social programming only allowed me to see with physical eyes, but now I could experience with spiritual eyes.

Many think you must see things to believe it. I know now I need to *believe* it in order to see it.

In other areas of my life I began noticing how I was able to create what I wanted in my relationships, health, and career. I had learned how to *be* in my life, and I am surrounded today with relationships that feel more meaningful and authentic. I'm more physically fit than I've ever been, and enjoy a career where I discovered a passion for writing. I love the life I am living and it just keeps getting better. I even manifested meeting Tony Robbins backstage at one of his live events!

When you can let go of people being right or wrong, the toxic energy of criticism and judgment will disappear, and a new space will open for you to be living authentically true with your heart's desires. Instead, let go of the need to be right. Understand that we are all doing the best we can given our experience, socialized beliefs, and knowledge. No one believes they are wrong, so when we make them wrong by criticizing and judging them, we only serve to condemn ourselves.

I stopped listening to the naysayers. I learned to quiet my mind so I could hear my own inner voice, instead of the programmed beliefs that didn't belong to me. I turned off the radio and limited the media that is saturated with criticism and judgment. And I listened to the people who were creating abundance in their lives.

As you embark on this journey, your existing comfort zone of friends and family may begin to hit some waves you might not be expecting. As I began to step more fully into who I am, I didn't realize that sharing this new me would challenge the established norm. I was growing and changing, and some of my friends and family not only didn't resonate with this new path, but openly criticized and judged me. I felt my old familiar world at odds for the first time as I established new roots. Overall, I felt more grounded, and it led me to a new world that resonated more strongly. I began attracting people who were more open and with whom I felt more connected. Soon, I found myself living in two separate worlds.

Along the way I have learned some really tough lessons:

1. I could no longer share everything with existing family and friends: Many not on this path, are unable to hear your truth without worrying, and will project their own fears with criticism and judgment of you. It can become toxic and you may need to walk away, or create two thought streams you manage.

2. Knowledge can prevent people from seeing the truth: The need to be right and wrong seeks answers in the form of 'outer proof' or 'knowledge' we use to justify that limits us from seeing all the possibilities, and living in true abundance.

We all have a unique light. It is not about being right or wrong. Nor is it about trying to fix ourselves or others. We are already perfect souls growing and changing along our individual journeys. When *you* become conscious to yourself, awakened to who *you* are, your light brightens and you attract the light of others.

You may work hard and *do* your life to achieve things; and you may still be living on the surface, while underneath that true sense of joy, fulfillment, and happiness eludes you. That was my life: I believed I was happy, only to discover that true happiness involved living more fully, *being* in my life experiencing both the laughter, and the tears.

If you are feeling like something deeper is missing, then I believe you are being awakened to who you really are. Slow down, notice what you are feeling inside for what matters to you, let go of *the* critical and judgmental thoughts of making ourselves and others wrong, and a space will open up for you to be authentic with your heart's true desires without worrying about what anyone thinks. From there, you can begin to start manifesting your desires.

About the Author

Carolyn Hidalgo, CPCC,

I have been on a journey of self-discovery and spiritual growth since I began doing my inner work in 2003, through the process of life coaching. It has transformed my life. I changed careers from being a chartered accountant to becoming a certified professional co-active coach (CPCC) with the Coaches Training Institute. What a ride it has been, and continues to be!

I am a wife and mother to twin girls and a son. I understand the challenge of raising children, managing a home, and developing a career, while striving to maintain your mental, emotional, physical and spiritual self. At the end of the day, it is about the choices I make, and whether they are in line with my values that allow me to live a life I love.

I have an enormous passion for connecting with people and love working with clients to create the life of their dreams. I have a vision to create a judgment free world, and a commitment to teach others how to let go of judgment to create deeply authentic relationships with loved ones in their life.

http://www.carolynhidalgo.com

POSITIVE PEACE

Primrose Oteng

For a really long time, I was completely enamoured with the idea of 'saving the world.' You are forgiven if you think that it sounds unbearably pious. However, in my own defense, I believe that many of us fall into the trap of wanting to fix a broken world. Perhaps due to the steady stream of bad news we hear about 'world doom,' I was convinced that my purpose lay in healing the world or its people in some way. So I resolved to 'saving people from themselves' and introducing them to a 'better way of life.'

Initially, I studied law because I wanted to champion the rights of the helpless. I lived for the show *L.A. Law* and dreamt of bringing corrupt politicians and heartless criminals to justice. But soon after I started practicing law, I realized that I couldn't bear the adversarial nature of courtroom proceedings. The night before court appearances, my stomach would be in knots as I imagined an irate judge giving me a public carpeting. So I took a break and never went back.

During a period of being rejected from just about every job I applied for thereafter, I had the time and the opportunity to become clearer about what I wanted. While my precise path remained elusive, I instinctively knew that I wanted to be of service in some way.

Almost naturally, I began to focus my attention on international politics and how I could have an impact on a global stage. They say that when you are clear about what you want, the opportunities will appear. Soon thereafter, the perfect opportunity presented itself. I was offered a job working on the political negotiations aimed at ending the war between the Government and the rebels in the Democratic Republic of Congo.

This experience offered me many things, including firsthand exposure to international negotiations and diplomacy. However, far more fundamentally, I learned that 'saving the world' would not be easy, especially because not everyone wanted the same things. That notwithstanding, I still looked at life very much in black-and-white terms – I was determined to use the forces of good to overcome the forces of evil.

After four years working on the Congo peace process, I left tired but not defeated. Because I felt such a strong pull to the work that I was doing, I knew that it had to be the right thing for me to do, so I continued.

Next, I moved to Sudan, where I worked on monitoring the implementation of the peace agreement signed between Northern and Southern Sudan, and the ongoing negotiation process concerning the Darfur region in Western Sudan. Even before my arrival there, I suspected my profile fit that of the 'perfect crusader' – I wanted to reverse the terrible images of suffering I had seen on T.V. and win a moral victory for the people.

Through my powerful imagination and the strong feelings I harboured about ending human suffering, I soon found myself in my 'dream job.' I had access to high-level political players in the global arena, and I was convinced that by working together, we would finally manage to create sustainable peace, at least in one region of the world at a time.

After working on peacekeeping issues for over a decade, including as part of the United Nations, here is what I now believe to be true:

1) Nobody needs to be saved, regardless of how helpless they may seem. When something goes wrong in our lives, we are each capable of saving ourselves.

2) Even in places where war has broken out in the world, and the lack of well-being seems so acute, the local capacities to create peace exist. As people, particularly external actors, we need to learn to stop trying to export our visions for peace and put national actors at the forefront of their own peace efforts.

3) Engaging only (or mostly) outsiders to broker peace tends to make members of the local population dependent on expensive international presences that cannot be sustained.

4) Our current approaches to forging world peace are almost entirely negative. They involve dissecting what has gone wrong with a view to redressing historical imbalances and grievances. As a result, opposing parties become even more mired in conflict as they seek to blame each other for what went wrong.

The more powerful of the parties may become focused on political survival and may make small concessions under international pressure that they have no intention of honouring. On the other hand, those attempting to win a bigger piece of the pie become so distracted by the injustices they have suffered, and what they don't want – that they fail to form a clear vision of what they do want. In the end, their lack of a clear purpose usually leads to their detriment.

5) Despite what many leaders claim, only few of them actually represent the true will of the people. While many of us like to believe that we can deliver the oppressed, in fact, as human beings, we are inherently selfish, and we can only ever effectively pursue our own interests.

6) However appealing an ideal – including global peace – might seem, it is never universal. The world is far too diverse for that, and there will always be people who have more to gain by waging war than by pursuing peace. Trying to force everyone to want the same things is futile. The more we try to coerce people into complying with 'accepted norms,' the more intransigent and powerful they become.

7) The world is not broken and is not in need of fixing. Even in countries at war, there are people who continue to live normal, even happy, lives – far happier than some who have never known war or have lived in prosperity. The problem is our focus. It has become so skewed that we fail to recognize or acknowledge any positive progress.

We also tend to judge people by our own standards, of what should make them happy or unhappy. Happiness is always an inside job – only we can determine what makes us happy.

Not only are we each born with the desire to be happy, but we are capable of fulfilling it. Our greatest satisfaction comes from realising our goals through our own genius. Yet sometimes, when we're doing well and we see others who are not, we feel guilty and attempt to redress the disparities by doling out assistance. But just how effective is this?

Think back to the last time you tried to alleviate someone's plight. Did you give money to a cash-strapped relative because you feared their kids would starve? Or did you 'solve' the problem of a friend who was in dire straits? How long did the effects last? I'm willing to bet, not very long. Your relative probably still needs cash bail outs, perhaps on a more frequent basis, and your friend may now be engulfed in a series of crises that have started to detrimentally impact your own life.

It is instinctive to want to end human suffering where we see it, but consider your own situation – what process did you use to improve your life?

Think about the last time you were filled with pride upon achieving something great. Without exception, your feat began as a mere thought, which you nurtured through burgeoning excitement, until your vision became so inspiring that you were compelled to act on it. And the success followed.

If you've had multiple successes, you have probably also increased in confidence and realised that you really can achieve anything, no matter what the odds. Statistics are for people who are looking for excuses. The evidence points to the fact that we can be, do, or have anything we set our minds to. Yet if some can do this, why can't we all?

Actually, we can. The day this realisation dawned on me, I suffered something of an existential crisis. I wondered what I was good for if it wasn't to champion someone else's cause. But it was also incredibly liberating to realise that we are each responsible for how our lives turn out and that none of us needs to agonise over how to rescue others.

Seeing people as incapable of rising above their challenges implies that they are somehow 'lesser than' we are; after all, if we could overcome life's obstacles to arrive where we are, why shouldn't they? I have stopped seeing people as weak and needy. Instead, I have developed an awe of human potential, as well as an unwavering belief in our inherent capacity to be great. *Instead of fighting to impose world peace, I have come to believe in the creation of 'Positive Peace.'*

After ten years of searching for solutions to political problems, including those that resulted in war, I now realise that in order to be sustainable, peace should always be predicated on the realisation of personal power.

What do I mean by personal power, and how do we access it? If I had to reduce it to basic principles, it would consist more or less of the following:

1) Human beings enjoy unlimited power, which we access through our minds. We create through our thoughts, and positive thoughts create positive realities. The way we feel indicates whether our creation will be positive or negative. To create a great life, we need to regularly cultivate positive feelings, including through practicing appreciation.

2) Cultivating positive emotions helps us to devise solutions to apparently intractable problems. Positivity broadens our minds, leading us to be creative and to devise win-win solutions.

3) People who are suffering have the greatest desire to end their own hardship (particularly in countries at conflict). They can do so through, amongst other things, the use of positive thought processes. Suffering inspires mental clarity about what we want and the motivation to pursue it. That is why our greatest triumphs often follow our darkest moments.

4) While there is a place for external assistance, such assistance should be based on the ability of communities and the individuals within them to decide and alter the course of their fate.

5) *Allowing* people to improve their own experience is an empowering process, while *rescuing* them creates dependence and, oftentimes, resentment. We all want to experience the feeling of invincibility that comes with creating something amazing, of proving that we are the captain of our fate, the master of our soul.

6) In providing service to others, we should view it as 'co-creation,' rather than 'us doing for them.' More fundamentally, such service should bring us joy and shouldn't feel like a burden. If it does feel onerous, it doesn't do anyone any good.

7) We need to focus on what works as the route to peace. While we shouldn't ignore our differences, we needn't over-emphasize them. Often, we have more points of convergence and can use them to create even greater harmony. *What we focus our attention on grows.*

8) We each need to be our own leader and follow our own movement. Don't give anybody else the credit for how your life turns out.

Starting today, vow to reclaim your power to create an awesome life. Cultivate a positive, personal peace. Once you realise that there is nothing that you cannot be, do, or have, you will not need to fight with anyone. There won't be any need for war. Let this be your greatest contribution to global peace.

About the Author

Primrose Oteng is the Managing Director of the Positive Peace Project (PPP), an organisation dedicated to helping individuals and organizations foster positive change through personal empowerment.

She holds a Masters in Applied Positive Psychology (MAPP) from the University of Pennsylvania (2008); an LL.B (Hons) from the London School of Economics and Political Science (1998); and a Postgraduate Diploma in Law from the Inns of Court School of Law (1999).

From 2002 to 2011, Ms Oteng worked for the United Nations Department of Peacekeeping Operations (DPKO) at the UN Mission in the Democratic Republic of Congo (MONUC -2002-2004); the United Nations Mission in Sudan (UNMIS- 2005-2007); and the United Nations-African Union Mission in Darfur (UNAMID – 2008-2009). She also served as the Assistant Chief of Staff of UNMIS (2010-2011).

Ms Oteng's work has taken her to several countries including Angola, Eritrea, Ethiopia, France, Nigeria, Portugal, Rwanda, South Africa, Sweden, Uganda, the United Kingdom, and the United States, amongst others.

She writes a popular column for Botswana's Sunday Standard newspaper; and is regularly featured on national radio where she shares empowerment strategies with a wide audience.

She was born in Gaborone, Botswana; and is fluent in English, French and Setswana.

http://www.positivepeaceproject.com

BLESSINGS OF ABUNDANCE

Fred DiDomenico

As I sat in my home office taking phone calls from clients, my thoughts and distractions overwhelmed my mind of how I am going to manage working and sustaining my home and family life, as my wife lay in our bed upstairs dying from cancer.

She had been fighting the disease for just over a year with what we thought was great success. We thought she was going to have a new life. Within a short time though we discovered her disease metastasized from her breast, throughout her liver and spine, and was spreading like wildfire throughout her body.

As her body melted away, she was dying fast while she grasped for life in bed every day.

At the time I was travelling and teaching seminars on the weekends, taking me away from home on a regular basis. As a chiropractor, my seminars are about teaching chiropractic doctors how to treat patients to better health with a spinal rehabilitative technique that returns youth, strength and healthy posture for life changing benefits. During the week I coached doctors to use these systems to build success in their practice.

Working from home, I had the advantage of being with my wife much of the time. The irony was that I taught doctors how to inspire patients to reach optimal health, yet my wife was dying of a fatal disease.

I wished for years she would have had the inspiration to help herself. We argued incessantly about this fact. Although I didn't agree with her choices, she taught me how to love her unconditionally. This was my greatest lesson and one of her greatest gifts to me.

147

I was now enveloped in the contradiction of how I could stay home with my wife to nurse her to her death, while giving up travelling and teaching seminars, which brought in the majority of the finances that paid for our life.

My worst nightmare was to be out of town teaching when she died, with me not by her side during her last breath to see her through her transition. I knew I would carry that regret for the rest of my life, and that was not the life I could live with.

On the other hand, if I lost the income and stayed home with her, I couldn't pay my bills, mortgage and risked the financial safety of my family and home. She had made up her mind to allow the disease to overtake her body to her impending death, and I felt the responsibility and love to be with her to her passing.

The time frame of her final breath remained unclear. It was possible for her to pass any day, or continue to resist the transition process, as she was afraid to die and leave her two children and newly born grandchild.

As I sat at my desk that day, my mind was overflowing with thoughts and stress because I knew in my heart what I was being called to do. The right thing was to stay by her side through the whole process, and in spite of the condition the world was showing me, it was time to reach inside myself and find unwavering faith.

I was raised in an Italian catholic home with strict religious rules. Although my family followed these rules, we were also raised with very spiritual practices. I was taught that God was protecting me and I could call on Him when I was in need of anything in the world. As stated in our Lord's prayer, *"...give us this day our daily bread..."* it was time to call on 'His daily bread' and put into use the spiritual principles I was raised with, my faith.

I had called on Him at other times in my life when conditions seemed tough or had proven to be very discouraging. When I had faith with confidence my needs were always met. I referred to these times of my past now as a reference to begin to draw my inner strength.

Here's one of my experiences...

Years earlier I had been going through a tough and emotional divorce. I was in church one Sunday standing next to my soon to be ex-wife during individual prayer as a congregation. I stood there in *so much* emotional pain with the process we were beginning. I could feel *deep* aching pain in every cell of my body, thousands of times worse than the deep aching pains you experience when you are sick. As I stood there with my eyes closed, I prayed with fervor, passion, even desperation, for God to help me and show me the way, begging Him to ease my pain.

All of a sudden my spirit left my body. I was no longer standing in church. I was now standing in an amazingly bright light. The light was so bright it was like the sun, yet it didn't burn my eyes when I looked into it. As I looked into this amazing light, the silhouette of Jesus appeared in front of me. He was only a silhouette because the light emitting from Him was so overwhelmingly bright, yet I recognized Him as if we knew each other and were coming together again. The love within the light was so great; it was not a love of this earth. It was the most amazing, heavenly, unconditional love I have ever felt and have yet to feel again. The power of this love and authority was so intense.

Due to my lack of self-esteem at the time, I didn't feel worthy to be in His presence. This was my own interpretation. I immediately fell to my knees with my head down to praise Him as I submitted to His glory. While face down in front of Him, I reached my right hand out and touched His flowing gown by His feet. My right second finger touched His gown and in that split second I felt a lightning bolt of energy shooting throughout my whole body.

I was electrocuted by our Lord, only it didn't feel like a shock.

It was an intense, powerful energetic charge. At that instant I suddenly opened my eyes and was standing in church. I was amazed to discover my physical body never left because I was not spiritually present. In amazement, I looked around to see if anyone noticed I was gone. Soon, I discovered that it was possible no clock time had actually passed. I was still standing next to my wife and she didn't notice anything different. I brought my attention back to myself and noticed all my pain was gone!

I felt amazing. I was happy, peaceful and all my physical ailments had disappeared.

I had manifested Jesus Christ and was healed.

That memory was the one I recalled at this time of my life when once again I was in crisis. I had many spiritual experiences in my life, yet that was the memory that stood out then, and it prompted me to remember that Christ is always with me.

With this experience to draw from, I knew in my heart I was being called to stay home with her. We were being given the opportunity to heal our lives and relationship in God's presence and he would provide all things.

I made a very straight forward prayer.

As I talked to God I said, *"If you want me to stay home God, then you are going to have to provide all the money and things we need to get through this."* That prayer felt more like a demand, yet I knew I could not make it happen according to the world. I was asking for, even demanding, a miracle.

I brought out 'The Abundance Book' by John Randolph Price, who writes about a '40 Day Prosperity Plan'. I used this book as a reference to confirm daily affirmations that remind us that God is the Source of all abundance, and to look to Him rather than outside conditions. I also began to tithe 10% of all my income, even though I was financially incapable of paying my bills. On top of this pressure, I added 10% to give away.

Tithing is a spiritual principle of success taught since the beginning of time. It also stated in the Bible, *"...prove me now this, says the Lord of hosts, 'if I will not open for you the windows of heaven, And pour out for you such a blessing, That there will not be room enough to receive it." Malachai 3:3*

I had *proven* the Lord before with tithing when I had been in severe financial stress in previous conditions in my life and He had always delivered. In the past I had tithed money that would put me in financial duress, with me unable to pay my bills, if He did not return the money plus more in a hurry.

He had been faithful with me and now it was time to show my faith back to Him again.

Every day I read the affirmations and prayed with gratitude that God would deliver and meet all my needs with confidence. I would normally stress about money, fearing about future bills and events. I have read many books, listened to self-help and motivational CD's, speakers and studied many spiritual principles. They all advise praying with gratitude and *believing* you will receive that which you ask for. I have known this information in my head, and now was the time to know it in my heart. I was learning there was a big difference between head and heart. I believed I would be taken care of yet I followed the spiritual Law of Detachment discussed in 'The Seven Laws of Spiritual Success' by Deepak Chopra. I was comfortable with uncertainty. In other words I didn't know how, I just knew God was going to deliver everything I needed.

Over the next eight weeks more than $8,000.00 a month came to me from unexpected avenues. First, my mortgage company sent me a check for about $4500.00 for an overpayment (which I can honestly say I never actually paid), as well as an unexpected tax return for about $4200.00.

The next month I had a chiropractor friend call me and say he just sent a $6000.00 check for me to coach him. I had no idea he was even giving that a thought.

Additionally I had very dear friends and business associates donate $3,000.00 for my wife's celebration of life service. There were other smaller financial blessings during that time, each of which I would give thanks and gratitude to God for His faithful acts. Everything was paid and more.

The Universe is here to love us all when we give love, faith and gratitude first.

I learned we get what we focus on. During a time when there was no margin for error allowed in my mind, I learned we can connect with our spirit, rise up to the conditions and "say to this mountain, 'be removed and cast in to the sea,' it will be done." *Matthew 21:21*.

I, with the help of God and confidence that we would get what we believe, cast this financial mountain into the sea with no effort.

My wife passed on and we were all blessed with an amazing spiritual experience. It was this experience that helped me rid my Self of all the illusions of who we truly are and how we view our Self.

This journey led me to the development of *H.E.A.L.E.D.*™- *'A 6 Step System to Help You Discover and Fulfill Your Divine Purpose in Life.'* It is this and many other experiences that were my guide through the many challenging life conditions. It has become my life purpose to give people the tools to live a fulfilling life – the one they came to this life for.

About the Author

With a religious and spiritual upbringing Dr. Fred believed people were born into this life to fulfill a divinely ordered purpose. In his own journey to discover his life purpose he became a chiropractor. As he had the opportunity to witness thousands of people regain their youth, vitality and strength through spinal corrective therapy during 14 years of practice, he was called to yet a higher intention. He became a professional life coach and founded a personal and professional chiropractic coaching group, Elite Coaching. While teaching personal/spiritual growth principles, spinal corrective techniques and patient management systems, he has helped doctors all over the country achieve higher levels of success and fulfillment with patients in their practices.

Throughout the years of striving to be his best and help others to do the same Dr. Fred had to overcome many of his own life challenges. Through persistence and commitment he discovered the formula for a system to help people overcome their personal barriers to discover and live their divine purpose. This led to the writing of the book, *H.E.A.L.E.D.*™ This book is a tool that will help people all over the world live a more empowered and fulfilled life. This will be a purpose he will fulfill for the remaining of his days.

http://www.youarenowhealed.com

http://www.elitecoachingllc.com

http://www.chiropracticunited.com

QUANTUM BLESSINGS

Mary Ellen Jirak

Success in life could be defined as being in a state of joy and nonresistance despite any circumstance. It would be impossible to have a physical body and be in this state continuously. However, it is possible to be conscious enough to so seamlessly go from the asking phase of manifesting to a state of non-attachment and manifestation that people would believe you to be a miracle worker. The creation of any desire does not take hard work as we have long been taught. Rather, the work of manifesting is about persistent focus, detachment, and gratefulness. Learning to bless can set you on the path to being a quantum manifestor.

Discoveries from particle physics have created huge changes in how we perceive our world. While ancient spiritual masters have long suggested that light is a carrier of information, affecting the DNA of all life on the planet, there now seems to be a factual basis for this mysterious truth. The study of holograms demonstrates with certainty that light can both carry and 'remember' sophisticated information and transfer this information instantaneously. Within every part of the hologram resides the blueprint for its entirety and each part can recreate the whole. The implications of this are far reaching indeed. As a part of the hologram of life, each of us retains the wholeness of 'all that is' within us, albeit not entirely in focus. We all possess within our DNA the code for higher intelligence. Because of this we all have glimpses of knowingness we cannot seem to explain. This is the womb of miracles. It is likely that if a laser beam could be shined on any of us, the whole of creation would be visible.

The new physics helps us understand that matter may be only a series of patterns that are out of focus, and subatomic particles aren't made of energy, they are energy! The effect the observer has upon existence is even more astonishing. Research continues to suggest that the state of matter (whether a wave or particle) is changed by the observer. The father of quantum physics, Niels Bohr, showed that a particle only becomes a particle when it is observed by someone. What we observe changes as we view it. Even more amazing is research by Brenda Dunne and Robert Jahn that shows that our minds and intent can change the outcome of events. This means that through our conscious intent, we manifest what we choose to perceive, and that we can and do create our reality!

A new theory called Quantum Entanglement now demonstrates that instantaneous movement of objects is possible. Scientists create two photons from a single source which are perfect mirror images of one another. When one particle is spun the other immediately begins to spin in the opposite direction. This phenomenon occurs even if the particles are separated, whether it is by an inch or ten thousand miles. The particles immediately communicate with one another despite no 'seeming' connection. Not only does this tell us that energy is infinitely intelligent, it is also connected to all energy everywhere, and thus as energy ourselves, it is connected to us.

Blessing As a Manifesting Tool

Quantum Entanglement perfectly explains how the Law of Mind Action works and why blessing can be so powerful. The Law of Mind Action states what we think about we bring about or, like attracts like. When we choose to bless that blessing is always reflected back to us. We are each a thread in the universal tapestry. The act of blessing reconnects us with our source and reminds us we are all one.

An example of blessing as a manifesting tool is the story of an entrepreneur who disliked making sales calls. Whenever the business owner even thought of making client calls she would feel ill. She understood the power of blessing and decided to apply this practice to help her marketing. Rather than making sales calls, she began to make daily blessing calls. Without telling potential clients what she was doing when visiting them, rather than pitching her product, she would simply listen to them while silently sending them thoughts of unconditional love and blessing. Afterwards she would present a business card, yet she would only discuss her products if asked by the potential client, or if she felt that doing business together would bless the customer.

The results of the blessing experiment were astounding. She went from getting one or two clients a week to one or two a day. By refusing to sell she sold more. If the owner she went to visit was not at their business when she stopped by, she would speak briefly with the assistant, bless her/him and leave a business card. Most often the owner would call her shortly afterwards. The more she blessed others, the more she was blessed.

This businessperson then decided to apply the blessing idea to her retail store. During daily store visits she would imagine the shop and its shelves radiating with joy and love, see each customer blessed with peace and happiness. Soon her employees began to notice that the clients attracted to the store seemed happier and spent more money. Customers began to comment how much they enjoyed shopping there because it was so relaxing and peaceful. Within a year the business sold in four days for twice the asking price.

The key to this process is that the business owner was not blessing for monetary gain, her primary focus was on blessing and serving others. By blessing we open ourselves; we allow the greatest outcome for all to occur. When the only goal is blessing, success always occurs. Even if a sale didn't happen, there was success since the purpose, blessing, always happened. By clearing herself from attachment to a specific outcome other than blessing, she was able to connect with and attract all good. According to Eckart Tolle, *"If you get the inside right, the outside will fall into place."* Blessing will always help us get the inside right.

The Power of Release

What if you never reach the goals and desires you set for your life, can you be happy anyway? This is a key question to think about. Are you pinning your happiness on a future event? Being disappointed with life as it is not only blocks your happiness but keeps the things you believe will make you happy from manifesting for you. In fact, placing your attention on your unhappiness merely attracts more unhappiness. We get what we think about most. When our attention is centered on what we are lacking or what is wrong, we put ourselves in the position to receive more of the same – lack.

The solution is to become detached from needing the outcome.

155

You focus on your desires and release them, trusting the best outcome will occur. Obviously, this sounds easier than it is. As we focus on our dreams and desires, it is easy to become ego identified with them and feel we won't be happy without them. To avoid this it is important to never let our dreams and desires define who we are. The journey toward a dream must be as important as the arrival. Your willingness to release attachment to getting makes its arrival inevitable. Your detachment brings you to a peaceful state setting you in the flow. Therefore, the receiving serves to make your already happy life even more richly blessed, rather than it being the source of your contentment.

Embracing a Life of Abundance

Life is one endless possibility. We are in a constant state of change. Regardless of our lack of awareness of the great power we possess, even the slightest shift in consciousness can have huge and immediate impact.

We have long held to the concept of evolution. Things evolve over thousands of years, developing slowly. Yet science has long been aware of times in our evolution where there have been huge unexplainable shifts called 'punctuated evolution'; where evolution speeds up beyond what had previously been experienced. Now scientists recognize that time may be a construct of the mind, and that throughout what is considered time, there are moments where our future literally reaches back to us and pulls us forward. As these times of 'punctuated evolution' occur, part of our previous history (beliefs) which blocked us from seeing new possibilities are literally erased from our memory. A part of our 'seeming' past is deleted.

To change our world, be it on the macrocosm (the world stage) or the microcosm (our own life), we must first begin to think about it differently. Abundance is unlimited. Unlike the physical strain we have been taught to rely on ('No pain no gain belief system'), our striving becomes about learning to focus our attention. Manifesting is reliant on our ability to focus our attention on our intents rather than on 'what is.' Just like the two photons whose movement was affected by the other, regardless of distance, we shift the outcome of our lives through our intent. We shift our attention from our 'now reality', to the objects of our creation. The more adept we become at this, the more quickly we manifest our good. Jesus said this so plainly when he said, "Consider the lilies of the field, how they grow; they neither toil nor spin, yet I tell you, even Solomon in all his glory was not arrayed like one of these."

Obviously this does not mean we do not take action. It merely means that we act from *inner guidance*. As we do, we are led to the synchronicities that bless our lives, as we continue to bless all we encounter. Why, you might ask, do so many live in poverty if abundance is unlimited? It is because they have not been taught about, nor do they understand, the Law of Abundance. This is because there is great fear in the world that there is not enough to go around, so we must take what we can, lest it be taken from us. Fear sets up barriers against seeing the unlimited abundance that can be effortlessly accessible to all. Until that fear is broken there will continue to be poverty and suffering in the world. As we let go of limiting thoughts and place our attention on abundance and blessings, we create the capacity for punctuated evolution and the breaking of bondage to lack in the world.

Abundance isn't something we must earn or become worthy of. Our work is to release the belief in lack, limitation, and unworthiness that has kept us bound and welcome abundance in.

What holds us back? FEAR—False Evidence Appearing Real.

As crazy as it may seem, we fear the unfamiliar, for even though our present circumstance may feel uncomfortable, it is familiar and known. This is less frightening than the unknown. We fear that in letting go of what we have come to know and expect, we risk losing all. Reluctant to take the risk, we mourn its lack rather than let our good flow in.

Become a Quantum Blesser

When we choose to bless, it opens us to that willingness to see the highest and best in each person we meet and in ourselves. Since we are all connected, sending the energy of *love and gratitude* to anyone serves to bless ourselves as well.

To put you into the manifesting mindset, use this five step process:

B—*Breathe:* Breathe in deeply through your heart and out through your solar plexus. Allow all stress and tension to release and turn all your thoughts to your breath. As your body begins to feel relaxed, repeat to yourself, "I am sorry, please forgive me, thank you, I love you." Continue to repeat these words quietly or silently in your head as you continue to breathe deeply. It is from this quiet place that the seed of desire is planted in the fertile soil of potentiality. You now ask.

L—Let Go: This is the detachment phase of manifesting. Remember, when clear and focused intention is combined with detachment, anything can be attained because it is based on an undeniable belief in your inner power. Attachment comes from a poverty consciousness. Detachment frees us from past thinking which has knowingness to it, since it is connected to a past we are familiar with. Along with that familiarity is limited thinking. From detachment comes expansiveness and the power to create.

E—Erase Negative Thinking: Each time you catch yourself in negative thinking or sense yourself feeling anything but joy and comfort in your body, turn your attention to something that improves your feeling. Allow yourself to slowly work your way up the positive scale one-step and thought at a time. Don't expect to go from anger to joy in an instant. Use the cues from your emotional guidance system to help you change your thoughts. Forgive yourself for any negative thoughts and realize now is the only moment you can change!

S—See the Good in Yourself and Others: Start each day with a willingness to see each person as you know them to be, without their fears that mask their true nature. As the 'Course in Miracles' says, 'Everything is either love or a call for love'. When you hear the call, *be love.* If you forget, be willing to step into willingness again.

S—Stay Grateful: Gratitude is one of the most powerful tools we have for manifesting. As you hold your desire in mind, not only see yourself experiencing it, but express gratitude for receiving each gift even before you receive them.

Closing Thoughts

The gift of gratitude and blessing leads us to the practice of perceiving, speaking, thinking, and acting from the awareness of the sacred nature of all things. Abundance encompasses many things; material wealth, good health, energy and enthusiasm for life, joyful relationships, freedom, creativity, a sense of well-being, and peace of mind are all a part of it. Yet even if we have the experience of all these things we will continue to feel incomplete if we do not nurture the divine spark within us. Seeing your life as a miraculous expression of the unconditional love that you are begins with blessing. Blessing is abundance. May your life be continuously filled and blessed with love and light!

About the Author

MaryEllen Jirak is a highly acclaimed teacher and award winning author, educated in the science and psychology of human behavior. She holds a masters degree in special education and provides consulting, coaching, and workshops for organizations, schools and parent groups. Her book 'The Gift of ADD: Secrets to Transforming Liabilities into Possibilities' is now in its second edition. Her second book for teachers, 'Teaching outside the Box: Conscious Teaching for the Twenty-first Century' will be published soon. Every child is a natural genius and comes into the world with unique abilities. Properly nourished, these abilities contribute to the advancement and prosperity of our world.

http://www.gr8beginnings.com

REAWAKENING LOVE

Erica Goodstone

Although my interest in relationships began at a very early age, it has taken many years for me to recognize and own my truth about who I am and what I can offer to the world. From school teacher to professor to relationship healing expert helping men and women heal their bodies, relationships and lives through love – it's been one long and arduous journey.

When I was attending college, the career choices for women were quite narrow. We were encouraged to become a teacher, nurse or secretary. I chose teaching. Shortly after graduation, I was placed in a 'good' school in a 'good' neighborhood. It was an experimental school with a non-graded primary (three grades in one), no walls between classes, and one-way mirrors.

I felt as if I was in a fishbowl with no escape!

When I discovered one of my students literally hanging in the closet, I decided to bring him to the Principal's office. As I sternly walked beside him, the little pint sized, arrogant, 'man' burst into tears. I don't remember if we ever made it to the Principal's office that day, but I do recall thinking, "Is this all there is?" "Is this 'good' teaching position the fulfillment of my dreams?"

Fortunately for me, the principal of this school – in her quest to make a name for herself – behaved in a controlling, dictatorial and even abusive manner. Along with three other equally disgruntled teachers, I quit at the end of my first semester.

In those days, it was not acceptable to just quit a secure job that had a guaranteed pension for life. I was twenty years old and my mother literally yelled at me the entire weekend.

By Monday morning I had already found myself a new job as secretary to the president of a prestigious recording company on Fifth Avenue in New York City. I loved this job! I was with creative people and adults, I felt noticed and valued, and men invited me to lunch at exclusive restaurants and private men's clubs.

After work, I would often play tennis, and on the weekends I would regularly take trips, not having to worry about whether I had enough sleep to be able to discipline a room full of unruly children...

But then three events changed the direction of my life.

First, one day I happened to see my powerful, 'happily married' boss fondling and kissing one of his top female employees. As executive secretary, I had access to a list of all the salaries of everyone at this company. To my dismay, I discovered that this woman, who seemed to dedicate her life day and night to the company, was earning less than half the salary of several men with less than half her education. I decided then and there that I would not dedicate my life to building someone else's company. So when my well-meaning uncle told me, "Go back to teaching, it's the best job for a woman," I listened.

Although I would have loved a career in communication arts, that choice was brushed aside in favor of what I was actually doing almost every day – playing tennis. I realized that if I was teaching tennis and other sports, I could really enjoy that. So I returned to graduate school and also made up a year's worth of undergraduate credits. Within three years, I completed my master's degree and got a full time high school teaching position in health and physical education...

This new position only made me happy for a few years though.

One day I was invited to teach as an adjunct instructor at a local community college, where I sat in the cafeteria and socialized with deans, coaches and other professors. I found that to secure a full time college teaching position, I needed to get a doctoral degree. A casual acquaintance told me about a unique and cutting edge program in human sexuality, marriage and family living at New York University. After one year in that program, I became a full time assistant professor at the Fashion Institute of Technology/State University of New York, where I went on to become a tenured associate professor, then full professor, and eventually chair of my department. My twenty-five years spent at the college were mostly wonderful and memorable. We were like one big happy (although somewhat dysfunctional) family.

At one point though, teaching at this school could be described as a *Golden Coffin*. That's when I decided to take an early retirement, create a new life and build a business that would be my legacy to the world.

My original goal was to get my book published: *Love Me, Touch Me, Heal Me: The Path to Physical, Emotional, Sexual and Spiritual Reawakening* and to build a full time counseling practice, providing seminars and lectures around the country. Since I had maintained a part time private sex therapy and mind-body therapy practice throughout most of my college teaching years, I thought the transition would be easy. However, to my surprise, I experienced a sense of lost identity, not knowing for sure who I was or what I was meant to do when I could no longer call myself a professor.

When I left my secure teaching position in 2000, my book had not yet been published. In fact, it was not published until 2010, a year after I completed an eight-month mentoring program that once again changed the course of my life. I had signed up for the program because it promised to teach how to write a book in 12 hours or less. My book had taken me about three years to complete, and it was sitting in a file box, unpublished. Yes, this course taught me a lot about writing books, e-books, articles, blogs, flow charts and building a business funnel. An added bonus was the emphasis on the power of social media networking and marketing. Little did I know then that this would become a full-time learning experience, not unlike returning to college for an additional graduate degree.

For several years now, I have honed my writing and speaking skills as well as my true vision and purpose. I have developed deep and lasting friendships around the world, and continue to study and learn, having taken numerous mentoring and training programs to continually enhance my online business skills. Along the way, I had the good fortune to connect with a powerful online group called, Tribe Syndication Association (TSA), where I have learned that the true power of giving is the only true source of receiving.

Now, I am a Relationship Healing Expert helping men and women heal their bodies, their relationships, and their lives through love. My dream is to teach men and women the power of love… teach them that the first step is to *truly learn to love oneself* – so simple, yet so difficult for many of us. My vision is to guide and assist women to embody their '*Authentic Feminine Power*', and my goal is to guide and assist men to embody their '*Authentic Masculine Power*'.

In my many years of counseling men and women, individuals and couples, I have discovered that it is very difficult for women who feel unloved to soften and reveal their feminine vulnerability, sensuality and longsuffering, caregiving capability. I have also learned that it is very difficult for men who feel unloved to soften and reveal their sensitivity, empathy, gentle caring and very human need for contact, commitment and closeness.

When men and women feel unloved or unlovable or not good enough in some way, they will predictably become habitually distant, clingy and needy, or they will perform a typical distancer-pursuer dance with partners who will participate in that game.

When men and women try to be authentic, after years of not being authentic and hiding, their new behavior often seems awkward and clumsy. Just as learning any new skill requires time and practice to perfect, it becomes really easy to revert back to old, familiar, 'safe' patterns.

The most difficult point is when you move far enough forward that the old behavior patterns no longer work and you cannot go back, but your new persona, your new way of being in the world, has not yet evolved and gelled. This is a state of being that Fritz Perls, the originator of Gestalt Therapy, called '*The Fertile Void*'. An unfamiliar, confusing state of mind, this fertile void contains all possibilities and all potential.

Anything is possible if you choose to look forward, create a new future, and stop looking back.

Watch a baby, any baby, and you will observe pure potential. Babies are authentic. They express their needs without reservation. They give their sweet giggly smiles freely and they let their voices scream and their bodies writhe in anguish when they hurt. Sometimes we have to truly fall apart, suffer our own internal anguish, and then forgive our self and others in order to move forward in life.

If you are afraid to fail and let yourself feel the inevitable pain and suffering in life, you will also be unable to succeed. Talk to anyone who has truly succeeded in business, in art, in long lasting intimate relationships, in sports, or in healing and recreating health. One pattern will become evident: the willingness to persist despite the obstacles, despite the pain and suffering, despite the opinions of others and despite their own doubts and insecurities.

If your relationship has been asexual, hostile, and unfulfilling for years, there may be a pattern of interaction that both of you have created together. If you have been single for years and cannot manage to connect in love, there may be a pattern that you have developed to keep love away. There *is* a solution. There *is* a possibility to recreate oneself, to recreate love with a partner, and to rediscover the joy of life and love, with or without a significant other. It all begins with love, learning how to acknowledge, appreciate and love oneself first and then to acknowledge, appreciate and love others.

At this point, I am finally living the life of my dreams. I am slowly building my global *'Healing Through Love'* mentoring programs. I experience joy and delight every time I observe individuals and couples turn from depression, hostility and isolation to those tender feelings of affection, desire and pure empathic love. I know, from personal experience and direct observation, that *love is the answer and the key to living a happy and fulfilled life.*

About the Author

Erica Goodstone, Ph.D., is a Relationship Healing Expert helping men and women heal through love. Author of *'Love Me, Touch Me, Heal Me: The Path to Physical, Emotional, Sexual and Spiritual Reawakening'*, she is also a syndicated columnist with hundreds of articles about healing, love and relationships published on such sites as ezinearticles.com, examiner.com, yourtango.com, and selfgrowth.com, as well as on her blog (1).

As a Licensed Mental Health Counselor, Dr. Erica helps clients to reconnect their mind and body, heart and intellect, and to recover their passion and purpose in life. An AAMFT nationally certified marriage therapist and AAS-

ECT nationally certified sex therapist, she is a diplomat for the American Association of Integrative Medicine, the American Academy of Pain Management and the American Board of Sexology.

You can contact Dr. Erica at her website (2) to find out more about her upcoming programs and get her complimentary report entitled: *Relationship Success.*

http://www.CreateHealingAndLoveNow.com/blog (1)

http://www.DrEricaWellness.com (2)

THE NEW CAR

Marlyse Carroll (alias Gabrielle)

"We definitely need a new vehicle, a medium-sized four-wheel drive," said Michael.

He was right. The car they had been driving for a few years had become inadequate for the growing needs of their business. It was too small to carry the amount of equipment needed to run personal development workshops and not powerful enough to safely tow a loaded trailer.

"Yes, good idea," added Gabrielle. "We are pretty good at manifesting. Why don't we choose the car we want and just manifest it?"

"Why not? Let's do it."

To Gabrielle and Michael, the matter was settled. All they needed to do now was to become very clear as to which vehicle they wanted and take appropriate physical and metaphysical actions in order to set universal forces into motion. They fully trusted that they would own a bigger and better car by the New Year without having to borrow money to buy it. They would simply receive it because of the fair exchange of energy between what they offered the world and what they asked for.

Gabrielle and Michael ran their business, the 'Inner Peace Institute for Wellbeing', on a financial shoe-string and yet they had never felt a lack of anything for very long. Whenever they needed assistance, goods or equipment in order to carry on their mission, the Law of Attraction worked in their favour and provided what they wanted. Sometimes a chain of events obviously followed consciously held decisions, at other times synchronicities seemed to unfold as the result of a fleeting thought. Even though Gabrielle was often surprised by their 'luck', she realised that the basic prerequisites were always there: *clear intentions, trust in the Universe and underlying feelings of gratitude, happiness and joy.*

That same evening, after Michael finished teaching his meditation classes, he noticed a book of raffle tickets sitting on the bench of the 'Inner Peace' meditation room and checked what the first prize was. Yes, it was a medium-sized four-wheel drive of a well-respected brand, a car he liked very much and had often admired on the road!

"What a beautiful car" he thought, "Just what we need. I love it, let's go for it!" There were five tickets left in the booklet. So he bought them all and straight away returned butts and money to the charitable institution which had organised the raffle. "Of course, one ticket would be enough," he later said to Gabrielle, "but I couldn't honestly ask other people to buy the last four knowing that they don't have a chance because we'll win the car!!" His tongue in cheek remark made her laugh.

That night, Michael and Gabrielle organised their plan of action. The draw was to take place three weeks later on the 24th of December at a local shopping centre. It was the first time that they had asked for something of substantial financial value, and they both felt as excited as eager kids writing to Santa. In fact, the analogy of children and Christmas was one Michael often used to explain the secret of manifesting. "You have to truly believe that what you want is already there for you, even if you cannot see it with your physical eyes. Imagine that you are a child who wants a red mountain bike more than anything else in the world and you discover that your parents have just ordered it for Christmas. Your dream bike is still at the shop, you haven't put your hands on it yet, but you know it's yours!

When you can feel just like this child, buzzing with excitement, happy in every moment, feeling love and gratitude, anticipating the most wonderful time because your current wish is getting fulfilled, you have put the cosmic delivery mechanism into motion. Your next step is to sustain this joyful, trusting energy until your desire manifests physically, because interfering negative thoughts or feelings will just cancel the order."

So the very next day Gabrielle and Michael went to test drive 'their' car. They instantly agreed on the colour it was to be, a bronze shade of metallic gold. Gabrielle took a few photos of Michael at the wheel.

As soon as they got back to the office, Michael installed the best shot as a screen-saver on his computer and Gabrielle kept a hard copy of the same photo on her desk, so she could subliminally see it all the time.

"Now that we know what this car looks like, feels like, smells like and sounds like, let's meditate on it," said Gabrielle. So from then on, they meditated together for an hour every morning. They started each meditation by visualising themselves winning the raffle, signing papers, taking delivery of their new gold car and driving it everywhere. They saw themselves packing it to go to workshops and retreats or filling it with camping equipment for their bush holidays. Each meditation also included time spent in inner silence, in a space of no-mind where happiness is found without any reason whatsoever. As they tapped into their inner centre of joy, they aligned their personal vibration to the vibration of the field.

Gabrielle, who was more introverted than Michael, would have preferred to keep their plans to themselves, but Michael chose to tell the whole world. He informed family, friends, staff and students that Christmas Eve would see them winning the raffle. 'We've ordered our next company car from the 'Great Cosmic Dealership'," he jokingly said. "And we'll be there for the draw, count on it. No way would I be anywhere else when they pull our ticket out of the barrel!" Most of those he told just laughed and answered something sensible like, "Well, just give us a call when you've won it, OK?" Others jokingly asked, "When is the party?"

On the day of the draw, whilst driving to the shopping centre, Michael and Gabrielle focused their minds by repeatedly chanting the sound "Aaaahhhhhh". It is a sound meditation that they often do whilst driving because it is very calming, has an external focus and leads to greater awareness of the present moment. At some stage Michael said, "You know, whilst I fully expect to win this car, I'm not attached to it so I won't be disappointed if we don't." "I'm not even willing to consider the possibility that we won't," answered Gabrielle. She had never felt as confident about anything as she did about their win.

Half an hour later, on the 24th of December 2000 at 4 p.m., Gabrielle and Michael won the beautiful four-wheel drive they had wanted. It was the first time that either of them had attended such a draw, which proved a rather low-key event for everyone but them. The man who represented the 'Deaf-Blind Association' turned up at the shopping centre a few minutes before 4 p.m. dressed in casual shorts and a t-shirt. His sleeveless attire made it obvious to all present that cheating was impossible. The big barrel holding about 125,000 ticket butts was already there.

As onlookers waited for the decisive moment several of them bought a last minute $2 ticket, including Gabrielle. At 4 p.m. on the dot, all remaining butts were added to the contents of the barrel, which the man then rolled for a while. After a minute or so, he opened a small door and plunged his naked hand and arm into the midst of those thousands of butts, rummaging through them before pulling one out. The first ticket he drew was awarded the third prize, the next one got the second prize and the third ticket proved to be the one that Gabrielle had just bought five minutes earlier.

As the man slowly read the number, a wave of excitement rose through the small crowd of onlookers, because the winning ticket was part of a booklet from which many of those present had just bought their own tickets. "One... Two... Three... Zero... (five seconds elapsed)... Zero... (someone let out a gasp in the audience)... Gabrielle and Michael both knew they had the ticket number 123,001. They looked at each other and felt their hearts beating faster and faster! "... One! Ladies and Gentlemen, the winning ticket is number 123,001, M. and M. Carroll from Lower Templestowe."

"Yes," roared Michael. "Yes, yes, yes!!!" The rest is history, as the saying goes. Michael and Gabrielle jumped up and down for a while, simultaneously laughing and crying. Some onlookers warmly congratulated them, while others walked away, understandably disappointed at having been so close to winning without quite making it. The man who drew the raffle was absolutely delighted to meet 'his winners', as he said. He had been working with the 'Deaf-Blind Association' for thirteen years, he explained, and it was his job to organise and draw their fundraising raffle each year.

"The draw has been such an anti-climax every other time," he said to them, "because the winners have not been present. As I was driving down, I just thought how nice it would be to actually have the winners attend the event, to meet them face to face straight after I drew their ticket. This is just wonderful, thank you for being here, you've made my day!"

Well, this event certainly made their day too. What a Christmas present!

About the Author

"A number of years ago, I discovered that my life mission is 'to make a difference, have fun and help others do the same'. I've been on this exciting path ever since, hence my participation in Adventures in Manifesting." So says Marlyse, alias Gabrielle.

Marlyse Carroll is a meditation teacher, writer, speaker and artist of Swiss French origin who lives in country Victoria, Australia.

In 1995, Marlyse co-founded the Inner Peace Institute for Wellbeing, a non-sectarian educational organisation specialising in personal transformation. Today, her main role there is to train new teachers in meditation, spirituality and wellbeing. She also leads life-changing retreats and workshops.

Marlyse's first book is titled 'Am I Going Mad? The Unsettling Phenomena of Spiritual Evolution' (Inner Peace Publishing, 2007, second edition 2009). Now an Australian bestseller, 'Am I going Mad' has been described by Dr John F. Demartini (best-selling author of the Breakthrough Experience) as a "must read... truly a physiological, psychological and spiritual masterpiece for the sake of human evolution."

http://www.amigoingmad.com.au

http://www.innerpeace.com.au

http://www.chrysalisart.com.au

WHEN RULES PREVENT, REINVENT!

Victoria Fabling

The Universe contains a vast pulsing Creative Source, poised to answer all messages in the affirmative, in its own unique way and timeframe. We all know this and yet sometimes we seem to hit a wall of resistance. I'd like to share with you a few ideas on how to get over, through or around this wall by:

1. Learning how to speak 'Universal'

2. Accepting that every Earth rule has an exception clause

3. Using your exceptional talent to pulse your message directly to Source

I believe Earth will once again be a part of Paradise when we remember how to speak one language, which I call 'Universal.' All living organisms on Earth, and in the galaxies beyond, communicate with ease, even if they don't have a large vocabulary. Human behaviour is affected by planetary movement; animals know and try to tell us when an earthquake is imminent; pets reach out to lonely people and shower them with affection; stones and herbs volunteer their use for healing; water freely cleanses, and fire seems happy to transform us – especially when acknowledged in ceremony.

When children are left alone in nature, they readily pick up this universal language along with unlimited cosmic wisdom. Over the years I have asked many children to describe where they came from and only a few have looked puzzled. Many remember other star systems, as well as parts of our world they've not yet visited (in this lifetime).

I was fortunate to be the first-born and to have had very little distraction from other children before I went to school. All summer long I would go outside to play with five stones that lived in the outhouse.

Stones are supposed to sit patiently and be dense. At four years old I had no preconceived knowledge about what stones are supposed to do, so each morning I would place them at the bottom of the lawn and wait while they travelled up the hill to join me where I sat by the top flowerbed. I also remember staying absolutely focused on the process of racing my five 'mice' (as they needed exercise), and would take them back to their home when the intense silence was broken by the words, "Lunchtime, Victoria!"

They say the veil of forgetfulness is supposed to descend upon each child by the age of seven. I have refused to allow this to happen to me, and I do my best to be around young children and encourage them to keep believing that rules are not necessarily truth. That is part of the reason why I ask children to share what they remember about life, the Universe and everything.

We are taught all sorts of half-truths such as: there are seven chakras, seven colours of the rainbow and seven days in a week. These examples tie in with a pattern around the number seven and are not questioned by the masses. The Mayan culture interprets calendars differently, however, and I encourage you to check the new rainbow colours at the next opportunity.

Let's all experiment with what we are told,

For knowledge may not be wrong, just old!

The Universe does answer heart-felt appeals if we are ready to receive a reply from beyond our current belief bank. There was a period in my adult life when I relinquished my habit of talking directly to the Creative Source and tried instead to pretend I wasn't lying when repeating responses in church. This experiment clearly wasn't working for me as I was having frequent panic attacks.

When I finally surrendered and cried out, "What should I believe?" I received the immediate, booming answer, "The Truth is within *you*." The vibration coming into the house was such that an empty mug smashed in the bath, and a back-up visual of the same message appeared in gold letters in the ether as I lay in bed. *You* means you and me, *all* of us.

This message is *so* important, which is why, despite its intimate details, I share this story.

The truth is only limited by our ability to perceive an outcome.

If you were in a boat, totally lost at sea, without a supply of drinking water, what would you do? I read a story recently about how the survivors of a shipwreck, drifting in a lifeboat for weeks, imagined the sea water they were drinking came from a fresh lake, bathed in sunshine and surrounded by green pine trees. Their joint, accumulated knowledge told them they would surely die from dehydration, but they decided to throw this belief overboard. Faced with no other option, they talked 'Universal' and the Creative Source said "Yes, here's potable water."

After the Vietnam War, an orphan was found, by a reporter, living in the countryside with nature as his mentor. This boy played with insects in the same way I used to play with rocks. In the course of playing he had accidentally pulled a leg off an insect and noticed it grew back. When one of the boy's legs was shot off below the knee by a landmine, he applied the combination of memory and intent to his own half-leg, which grew back, just without a foot! The kicker is, insects don't have feet either.

The Creative Source develops the picture we offer.

In order to practise speaking 'Universal,' pick something which is beyond human each day, ask a question, wait and then act on the reply. Very often you will be led to a situation where you can help, and your reward will be another friend that thinks the world of you. This friend may be a tomato plant asking to be placed in a sunnier part of your kitchen, a bee with a crooked wing which would welcome some encouragement as it tries to fly, or a bird appealing to you to chase away the neighbour's cat!

By consistently speaking 'Universal' on the Earth plane, you will empower yourself because you will soon be able to connect directly with anything in the Universe. This includes weather patterns, beings in other realms and loved ones who cannot communicate in a normal way.

Imagine how glorious it would feel as you hold a vision of intergalactic harmony.

You may wish to take manifestation to a whole new level, becoming a co-creator of your personal dreams on and for a new Earth. Maybe you will also invent ways of treading gently which are unanimously accepted. To bring back Paradise, a place where the lion lies down with the lamb, we not only have to build our self-esteem, but also break the so-called, fixed 'scientific laws,' and replace them with unlimited love ones.

Here are two playful ways I use in order to by-pass any Earthly obstacles.

The Gingerbread Man

When I'd finished writing a fable called 'The Gingerbread Man,' I decided to embrace the manifestation technique he brought to my attention. Now, each morning, I pick a concept with the help of a pack of angel cards; draw an outline in the space in front of me of a life-sized Gingerbread Man standing for this concept. I then take a breath of intent and step boldly into that new energy field. As I am now transformed, I also have the power to pulse the concept I embody in circles around the Earth, should I wish to do so. The idea starts as a thrill in my heart, followed through with my conviction, and then I see and feel it working in my mind's eye.

Pulsing to and from Source

First I reclaim my power within the calm, intense silence, as I simultaneously focus on a worthy goal. I then increase my vibration with a combination of joy, absolute faith and excitement. I call forth the highest source of pure love and light energy and fill my whole body so full that my temples fairly burst. I then shoot this request out into space faster than the speed of light and through the sound barrier, so that it can be seen shining in the Milky Way. I wait for feedback in the form of an *inner yes* sensation (an involuntary smile or flow of relaxation) that my wish has the support of the Creative Source and give thanks.

Try using one or both of these techniques, perhaps adapting them to suit your personality. It is also possible to pulse down into the Earth from the cosmos and upwards from the crystal centre, using yourself as a conduit, in a cyclical way. You may feel electric afterwards, will definitely glow, and probably start to 'youth' depending on the frequency of your practise. I would only caution you not to send the message from your heart; hold the intention there, but let your

Higher Intelligence deliver the pulse wave from your crown or your feet. Meditation circles are perfect for this exercise because others can magnify the energy and look for the light shining in the cosmos.

About the Author

Victoria Fabling became a writer at the age of eight when she wrote and illustrated her first book, 'Woodland Friends.' Subsequent books have shared the fable theme, using non-human characters to illustrate human lessons.

Beauty and justice have been her prime motivators, and as a young adult she joined the fashion industry, thereby fulfilling one of her passions. She later graduated as a graphologist and represented people who were wrongly convicted for signing documents. In 1991 she started training as a healer and mentor with 'The Healing Trust' and since then has incorporated all four careers into one.

Victoria was raised in England and moved to Canada in 1998, where she has been sharing her substantial knowledge of the metaphysical world, and writing. Her way of teaching is child-like and she loves being outside in nature, embracing the innate wisdom within everything. She is essentially a pantheist, someone who believes there is a Universal Intelligence which lovingly supports us all. Wordsworth's 'Intimations of Immortality' describes this concept beautifully.

Victoria can be reached through her websites and, if you like her story-telling style, can ask her to compose a personal fable. She travels internationally with her work, and is grateful to have the Internet as her office door.

http://www.myspiritualmentor.com

http://www.fablingsfables.com

CONSCIOUS DECISIONS

Carol Kelson

The last six months of my senior year in college were extremely challenging. I lost my boyfriend in a car accident while he was driving home after visiting his boss in the hospital. An oncoming truck hit his car and both he and the passenger died. A few months later, my best friend, suffering from a cold, wanting to sweat out his sickness, decided to play a couple games of basketball with his friends. That night he went to bed and never woke up. The virus entered his heart while he was sleeping. Only a few months after, my current best friend's brother died in a car accident when the car flipped over.

These three incidents happened within a short period of each other and left me dumbfounded and depressed. This was the opposite of manifestation. It was life beyond my control. It was having the rug pulled from under my feet and left me groveling on the ground, without a map telling me where to go. I was in disbelief and despair. Hadn't I done everything I could to be a good person? I had spent Sundays leading a church youth group. I served the elderly and the homeless. I didn't drink, do drugs, or party. My irrational belief was that being 'good' would spare me from life's tragedies. Why did I believe that harm's way only came to those who did harm? Hadn't I suffered enough in my life already growing up with a mentally ill brother? Wasn't there a quota somewhere in heaven, in the Universe, that only allowed for so much pain in a certain amount of time? I felt my quota had been exceeded and life made no sense to me at all. What was the point? Why work so hard to do good in the world when it would only lead to so much suffering? I was angry at God and shut down.

Forgoing graduate school, I felt lost and directionless. I stayed in Los Angeles, California, working long hours as a means of forgetting about the pain. It was through work that I met my husband who gifted me with two beautiful children; first a boy and then a girl. Though my relationship didn't last with my husband, this chapter will explore manifesting a lasting healthy relationship with your children, and even your former spouse. I suppose there are many things one might want to manifest, including fame, fortune, and good health. All these manifestations are valuable and worthwhile. However, my desire was to manifest children who could be happy, resilient, and good people, giving back to the world despite their life circumstances, in this case, divorce.

Coming from a shame-based culture with very few divorces in my extended family, it was not an easy choice. In addition, my children attended a private school with very few divorced families. This added additional pressure, as I would now stand out as being different, my failure expressed. I remember hearing a story about a despondent man sitting in the doctor's waiting room with his kids running wildly about, screaming and making loud noises as they jumped on and off chairs, disturbing other waiting patients. The patients spoke amongst themselves, "Why is the man so irresponsible? Can't he manage his own children? What is wrong with him?" Finally, a woman frustrated beyond her limits approached the man and adamantly stated, "Sir, can't you get a hold of your children? They are being rude and disturbing the others in the room!" The man, looking up slowly and apologetically quietly responds, "I am so sorry. My children have just found out that their mother has died and I am lost in sorrow." As judgments were thrown upon this man, I too had judgments thrown upon me as a divorced mother with two small children.

Not wanting to talk about the details of my divorce, I gave others fertile ground for making assumptions and passing judgment. My goal was to put the emotional needs of the children first and I knew on some level this meant avoiding divisive conversations and sending no ill will or harm to their father. In the long run, I wanted my children to be happy and for them to have a loving relationship with both parents. I knew research showed that kids fared better over time if they have the loving support and involvement of both parents. I wanted this for my children, even if it meant dealing with my own anger and disappointment in more difficult ways. My goal was not to hurt my former husband; my goal was to be happy and to raise happy children. In the meantime, if my former husband could also be happy, that would be all the better for him and the kids. Happy parents make for happy children.

However, I am *not* advocating for divorce. On the contrary if, as a couple, things can be worked out, it pays off financially and otherwise to stay together. Only those in the 'fraternity' of divorce know how painful and difficult, on so many levels, divorce really is. However, in circumstances of seeming impossibility, I am not here to judge. For me, I had become a walking dead person. I knew I was not an inspiring example for my children. I was better to my children when I had something to give. Under those circumstances, I was downcast, depleted, and giving only what I could from my reserves. I had no idea how I would manifest happy children when I myself had lost my way. So I started reading. I read book after book, making sure I could be the best parent given the circumstances. I read parenting books, divorce books and self-help books. I prayed. I prayed every day, afternoon, and evening constantly asking for guidance and most of the time help. I worked on myself, taking responsibility for how I contributed to the situation and how I could help myself despite it.

As a parent, I wanted to stay active in my children's life, so I went back to school to work in a field that would allow me the flexibility to be available to my children. During those years in school, I learned life lessons that help me to this day. For example, I now realize my upset is just that; *my* upset. No one else causes me to be upset. It is my choice as to how I react and respond to circumstances. If I do not react and respond in a way I like, it becomes my job to alter my response. It was time for me to stop blaming and take responsibility for that which I could control. I realized I can't control others, but I can learn how to control myself.

The next life lesson I learned was to see the loving essence in others, including my former husband. As good as it may feel to be in a position of righteousness, feeling right, in many ways, is simply feeding the ego and makes others angry. Instead, if I could see the loving essence in others, including those who have hurt, betrayed, or spoken ill of me, I could have peace knowing we are all on our own learning journey.

Perhaps the most important life lesson I learned was about forgiveness. Not only forgiving others, but more unfamiliar to me, forgiving myself. I spent the next few years working on forgiving my parents, my siblings, past boyfriends, friends, God, my former husband, and myself. Instead of holding on to judgments of how I believed others should have behaved and acted, including myself, I came back to the truth. The truth was that perhaps that was the best they could do at the time; perhaps that was the best I could do at the time. Perhaps we didn't have the tools, knowledge, education, or skills to behave any differently. Perhaps we didn't have good role models. Perhaps we had a bad day. Perhaps it was a time in our own personal growth. Perhaps there is a bigger picture that we don't completely understand.

Then I had to forgive myself for judgments I held of myself: for the pain divorce caused to my kids, my parents, my ex, my friends, my faith, my culture, and my family name. It was a time of feeling very alone. My friends, trying to hold their own relationships together all held their own various opinions: some believing it was God's will for me to stay in the marriage, and some feeling I should leave my husband and not allow him to have access to the children and everything in between. It was a time when I had to look deep inside myself and make choices I knew I would be responsible for and have to live with.

It was my kids who inspired me. I wrote out goals, not for myself, but for how I wanted to raise my children and what that would look like in five, ten, fifteen years. This was a little tricky because as much as I could hold a vision in my mind, I had learned all too well that ultimately we cannot control the lives of others. The three deaths in my senior year of college made that absolutely clear to me. What I did know was that I could do the best on my end and remain flexible. My kids are their own unique beings and even my best efforts cannot change the uniqueness of who they are, nor would I want it to. My goal was to embrace their uniqueness and support that uniqueness, allowing them to ultimately be who they wanted to be.

The times spent apart from my children were the most difficult for me. As hard as it is going through a divorce, being away from the kids was the worst part. This was especially true during holidays, but there were some bright spots to encourage me along the way. My divorce definitely made me closer to my parents. Although it was difficult for them at first, the way my parents jumped in and involved themselves with their grandchildren is a special gift that more than made up for any adolescent angst I had held against them. The love and care of grandparents is huge. Grandma and grandpa's house didn't change; it was the same as it was before. My kids could experience being loved and cared for without extraneous logistics.

They say you just need one person you can really talk to, to make it through okay in this lifetime. I was blessed with two! My kids, I am thrilled to report, are doing well in school, are fun to be around, and most importantly, are happy. My former husband and I have improved our parenting skills and as individuals. I am extremely thankful he is an involved father who deeply loves our children. We have a respectful, cordial relationship, free from verbal behind-the-back divorce poison and triangulating the kids. The end result: happy kids and healthy co-parenting. If there were anything I would want to manifest, this would be it. It's not all that I imagined it would be and it has not been easy. There were some rocky spots when I questioned how things would turn out. Fortunately, we all survived and hopefully are better for it.

When the divorce started my daughter was in pre-school and my son was in first grade. Our kids are teenagers now and I know the work is still not over. The work at manifesting healthy happy kids is an ongoing process.

If someone asked me what advice I would give to raise healthy, happy kids, I would say, take care of yourself, but keep your children your priority (especially above your ego, in whatever way that means to you). The second piece of advice I would give is to try as best you can to listen to your children's feelings. When feelings are heard and understood, people feel supported and safe. I find this means the world to children, no matter what age. It is not about left-brain fact finding and proving who is right that builds heart to heart connection; it is truly getting to the place of connecting with love.

Now that the kids are getting older, starting to drive, and sooner than I know will be leaving for college, perhaps I can start manifesting many other wonderful things in my life. For now, this journey of manifestation has been worth it and the journey is not yet complete. If you can stay married, then do everything you can to strengthen your relationship. A house divided is a lot more difficult than it appears. As parents having gone through divorce, we know the hidden secrets and struggles only those who have gone before us and with us know. However, if divorce is the best option because the challenges are insurmountable, do it in a way that puts your children, and healthy relationships, first. Work on yourself rather than blaming the other person.

Forgive and then watch for the miracles to appear.

About the Author

Carol Kelson is a practicing licensed Marriage Family Therapist in Beverly Hills and the Larchmont area. She works with individuals, couples, children, parents and teens.

Carol's strength lies in listening and talking to others, and understanding the curve balls of everyday life. She knows what it's like to juggle work, family, school, activities, and kids. She also knows what it's like to feel you are failing in many area of your life at any given time! The imperfect mom, Carol understands through family members, friends, her own experience and training, the pain of losing your loved ones, divorce, single parenting, coping with mental illness, trauma, and addictions.

Her current passion is supporting the people of Sudan and South Africa. She is working to raise financial donations to support community leaders in Africa working with the disenfranchised and implementing programs to heal trauma.

http://www.carolkelsonmft.com

THE SECRET SKILL

Jeff Gignac

Years ago, I was offered a big bag of money to do something that I believed was wrong and unethical. Now, you might be thinking that the "big bag of money" is just an expression or a metaphor, but it is not.

I was contacted by the CEO of a company who offered me a big bag of cold, hard cash to be delivered by courier if I would agree to purposefully destroy the reputation of a competing company, using the Internet.

I declined the offer, but I have to admit that it was one of the most difficult things I've ever had to do because I was desperate for money; my family was suffering.

Just six months prior to that offer, I had started a new business providing Search Engine Optimization (SEO) services because I was not making enough money as a clinical hypnotherapist and master practitioner of Neuro-Linguistic Programming (NLP). I had great clients, and I was doing seminars, but it just was not enough.

A few months after starting this new business, I started to make lots of money because I quickly became exceptionally talented at getting websites to show up high in the search engines, but it was still not enough to cover my back taxes and the massive debt that I so foolishly had racked up over the years.

The offer that this CEO made to me would have been easy for me to do. It would have paid enough money that would have solved ALL my financial problems. I am not proud of the fact that I actually took a day to think about it. I should have declined the work on the spot, but there was one other factor that made this man's offer a little more difficult to turn down. To fully understand this additional complication, I'll have to take you back in time just a little further...

One month prior to starting my new business, I had an epiphany that would eventually change my life forever. This epiphany turned into what I now call "The Secret Skill."

I call it "The Secret Skill" not because it has anything to do with the Law of Attraction or the book *The Secret*. It has nothing to do with those things. I call it as such because every millionaire I met used it, and almost all, if not every one of them, had no clue that this was the driving force for their continued success.

Over the course of my life and work experience, I had the opportunity to meet and talk with over a thousand millionaires and multi-millionaires. I had this opportunity mainly because of the nature of the work I did as I was putting myself through school.

I had always been fascinated with self-made millionaires because I was bound and determined to be like them one day. So every time I had the opportunity, I attempted to discover how these people became rich.

Over the years, I had compiled a massive list of skills, qualities, and traits that these men had. I spent years of my life acquiring as many skills and characteristics of these millionaires as I could, hoping that I, too, would become rich.

Well, it never worked.

And I was very frustrated with everything until I had an epiphany...

One day, as I was thinking about all the wealthy people that I probed for information, it occurred to me that there was one commonality between these people that I had never noticed before – each and every one of these self-made millionaires had become really proficient at applying *one* skill in their lives. The funny thing to note here is that many, if not all of them, did not even know that they had acquired this skill and were using it on a daily basis to achieve their wealth.

I discovered that these people had become really good at *achieving goals*, no matter what they were. This was the first time that it had ever accrued to me that *the ability to set goals and then achieve them was a SKILL* – something that could be learned, practiced, and eventually mastered.

That was my epiphany!

I had spent years trying to be good at all kinds of things because I thought they were what would help me become rich. In reality, these wealthy people became good at these things because they were the ones necessary to become wealthy based on their personal circumstances and situations.

This moment of clarity was both very exciting and troublesome for me. On one hand, I was very excited because deep inside, I knew I had discovered the missing link – the one last piece of knowledge I needed to become wealthy. If you think about it, you might get really excited, too.

If you master the ability to set and achieve goals, you can essentially write your own ticket and create exactly the life you want. There's no need to become great at everything; just become really good at 'getting good' at things and achieving goals, and you can do whatever you want in life.

On the other hand, I was also troubled by this epiphany because there was still one question left unanswered: how does one learn, practice, and master the ability to set goals and predictably achieve them?

After some intense research and lots of experimentation, I created what I believe to be a brilliant way to train, practice, and develop this skill very quickly.

I used it with my NLP and hypnosis clients, and it worked for everything. It worked so well that I started to use this system of training the "Secret Skill" paired with some focused goal setting almost exclusively in my practice.

I would teach my clients what "The Secret Skill" is and how to develop it, and once they became good at it (usually after a few weeks), I would have them focus on goals that once achieved would make it impossible for their problem to exist. For instance, I had one client who suffered from extreme anxiety and depression. None of my regular bags of tricks worked, so I asked her what emotions she needed to feel on a daily basis that would make it impossible for her to have anxiety and depression.

Once I got the answer, I taught her "The Secret Skill" and had her get good at it. I then had her set goals regarding feeling the way she wanted to feel. After four weeks, she had achieved her goals! She was able to feel the way she wanted to feel when she wanted to feel it, making it impossible for anxiety and depression to rule her life.

I also used the process to help my clients make more money, find better jobs, and get out of debt. Additionally, I used the process for myself, and quickly became really good at setting goals and predictably achieving them. I started to make more money than I had ever seen, and I felt like I could do anything.

The process worked with everything.

I started my new SEO business because the opportunity presented itself, and I quickly became so good at it that I found myself working with multi-national brands. I was pulling in so much money that I found myself only a couple of months away from being able to pay the mountain of debts I had.

It became easier and easier for me to achieve my goals, and eventually I started to get a little extravagant in my goal setting. Understand that I was making good money, but my family and I were still suffering because of all the money that had to go out. I sold my car, and I was working like crazy not to lose anything else. So I sat down one day and set a goal to have a big bag of money show up from one means or another. I used the words "big bag of money" in my focused goal statement. I was pretty certain that a huge sum of money would show up because of all the success I had so far, not to mention the success my clients were having. All this considered, I never actually thought A BIG BAG OF MONEY would present itself until that day it was offered to me.

This just blew me away, and I could not help but sit on the offer for 24 hours before I declined it.

After all, it was exactly what I wanted. Or so I thought.

I learned a really big lesson that day. While I wanted the money, I did not want it 'by any means necessary,' no matter the cost. Living the exact life I wanted did not include hurting myself or other people. It did not include behaving unscrupulously.

Today, I teach "The Secret Skill" as part of an entire formula called "Goal Factory," which naturally protects people from making the same error that I did. It's designed to help people live the exact life they want to live, whatever that means for them.

Getting rich or achieving anything at the cost of your relationships, your health, or your integrity is not going to make you happy. Living the exact life you want to live, on the other hand, will make you happy. So if you do take the plunge into The Goal Factory Formula, I simply ask that you follow it to the letter, so you too can live a happy and prosperous life.

About the Author

Jeff is a clinical hypnotherapist and licensed Master Practitioner of Neuro Linguistic Programming, and a expert in goal achievement. Jeff is also the co-founder of A.R.T. (Adaptive Response Technologies), Creator and innovator of numerous advanced Brainwave Entrainment Technologies that continue to revolutionize the field of personal development.

Currently, Jeff is working on new Brainwave Technology for stimulating and suppressing sub-dominant brainwave patterns as means to maximize various emotional, cognitive and behavioral outcomes.

http://www.goalfactoryformula.com

http://www.jeffgignac.com

SHARE YOUR STORY AND JOIN THE COMMUNITY

Have a Story to Share?

Everyone has a story, including you! With several *Adventures in Manifesting* titles in production each year, we are constantly looking for more journeys to share. Ask yourself- 'What story of mine could change someone's life?'

Whether you have a story to tell or lesson to teach, we're listening. Share yours and get the guide to writing and submitting your chapter here:

www.WhatAreYouManifesting.com

The stories we keep an eye out for are any that have to do with manifesting (success, spirituality, health, happiness, wealth, love prosperity, inner guidance, achieving dreams, overcoming obstacles, etc.).

If chosen as a top submission, we will get in touch directly to invite you to be a part of one of our next *Adventures in Manifesting* titles.

Looking for Guidance?

WhatAreYouManifesting.com is also a place to freely join a course & community with weekly lessons and daily action guides for manifesting.

By training you to develop rituals for success and creating the space to get the energy flowing, it will enable you to focus on your intentions from the purest place possible.

www.WhatAreYouManifesting.com

Join now to surround yourself with some incredible individuals. It truly is a place of joyful intention marked with the loving energy of gratitude and appreciation.

Feeling Inspired?

We always love to hear how our readers were touched, inspired or changed by the stories shared. If you'd like to share your experience, then you guessed it, hop on over to the WhatAreYouManifesting.com home page to let us know!

MORE ADVENTURES IN MANIFESTING TITLES

--iBooks and Kindle--

All Älska titles can be found through the www.WhatAreYouManifesting.com portal or requested from your local bookstore (and found through online bookstores as well).

<u>Books</u>

Adventures in Manifesting: Success and Spirituality

Adventures in Manifesting: Health and Happiness

<u>The Kindle and iBooks</u>

Each of the Adventures in Manifesting titles above can also be purchased via the Amazon Kindle or iTunes iBook formats via WhatAreYouManifesting.com.

SHARE WITH LOVE

Is someone you know on the deep and profound journey within? If so, be sure to share with them the entire book or specific stories you intuitively felt would resonate with them.

The meaning of Älska is 'to Love' (it's a Swedish Verb!)

The *chapters* were written with Love.

The *book* was published with Love.

And now it's up to you to *share* with Love.

From the bottom of our hearts and deepest depths of our soul, thank you, thank you, thank you.

With Love & Gratitude,

Älska

http://www.AlskaPublishing.com